TWENTY CENTURIES OF BRITISH INDUSTRY

TWENTY CENTURIES
OF
BRITISH INDUSTRY

HUGH BODEY

DAVID & CHARLES
NEWTON ABBOT   LONDON
NORTH POMFRET (VT)   VANCOUVER

ISBN 0 7153 6863 X
Library of Congress Catalog Card Number 75-10515

For Mary, with love

Set in 11 on 13pt Plantin
and printed in Great Britain
by Latimer Trend & Company Ltd Plymouth
for David & Charles (Holdings) Limited
South Devon House Newton Abbot Devon

Published in the United States of America
for David & Charles Inc
North Pomfret Vermont 05053 USA

Published in Canada
by Douglas David & Charles Limited
132 Philip Avenue North Vancouver BC

Contents

5

List of Illustrations

PLATES

Preface

There is a wide range of books on individual British industries, but there seem to be few of a more general kind that outline the growth of industrialisation in this country. Discussions with students and adult education classes have suggested that such a book could be helpful—and so the idea of writing it grew. While very much aware of the dangers of skipping around in other people's gardens, I hope the book may provide a useful introduction to more specialist books for some, and an aid to examinations for others.

The tale of industrial growth in Britain is very much a saga of human resourcefulness, determination and, all too frequently, brutality. It contains all the characteristics that make up individual people, for more sections of society are affected by industrial activities than by any others. If lack of space has forced the virtual exclusion of such matters as rates of pay, housing and factory reform, I hope the reader may yet be able to look on this book as, in some ways, the background of Everyman.

The book has taken shape over many years, so there are more people to whom I owe thanks than there is space to mention by name. I trust that teaching colleagues who explained technical matters, students who argued with my conclusions and school children who encouraged me by their enthusiasm will all regard thanks in general as being meant for them personally. Particular thanks are gladly given to John Whitaker for the maps and David Cockrell for the remaining drawings, to my mother who typed the manuscript and to my wife and children who have patiently looked after me while the book has been prepared.

Golcar, April 1974   HUGH BODEY

9

Note

This is a difficult time to write a historical book that must include weights and measures. Should they be historically accurate in imperial (and sometimes pre-imperial) units, and so be easier to link up with documentary and published material? Or should they be in the metric measures due to be in use shortly after the publication date of this book?

I have resisted the appeals of the Metrication Board in the belief that most readers will find the older measures have more value at present. Putting the metric equivalent of every figure would have made for extra detail in a book that was bound to bristle with facts, and would have required the exclusion of even more material to keep within the limits set.

1 Introduction

People are working in an industry when they are making more goods than they need for their own families, and can therefore sell or exchange these goods for others. The man who chipped flint tools in a prehistoric village and swapped them for pottery was as much an industrial worker as the handloom weaver in a cottage or the wage-earning fitter in a car factory. They are all using their abilities to make things that others want, and parting with them in a way that allows them to obtain what they cannot provide for themselves.

Farming could reasonably be included with the other kinds of industry. It is often omitted, though, perhaps because the farmer's work is very different from most other kinds of employment. He is principally concerned with living things, plants and animals, and his work is to a large extent controlled by the weather and the seasons. His problems are different from those of the industrialist, whose raw materials are either inanimate, or at least dead. Moreover, agricultural history is a vast subject in itself and any book that attempted to give equal coverage to agriculture and industry would need to be extremely long. However, these reasons for omitting agriculture are largely reasons of convenience; there is no fundamental difference between the two kinds of work, and they were combined successfully by most of the population for centuries.

Industries can be divided into three main groups: those supplying raw materials and power, those that use these to manufacture goods and the transport industries that distribute the goods. As with all attempts to simplify complex matters, there are some industrial activities that could fall into more than one category but these divisions summarise most industries. At the same time, these three groups are all interdependent; the blacksmith uses coal to forge picks for the miner, whose coal is then transported back to the forge. Most interdependence is more complicated than that, and has become increasingly complex since the early nineteenth century.

The level of industry in the country at any particular time is the result of many factors. The supply of raw materials is vital to industrial activity but is very variable, especially in the case of products, such as wool, that are derived from agriculture. So far as native mineral resources are concerned, supply depends at first on knowledge of their whereabouts before they can be extracted. The development of the North Sea oilfields is a case in point. Even when reserves of resources are known, it may be impossible to extract them at a reasonable cost—expansion of the Midlands coalfields was only worthwhile when canals and railways were built in the region. The availability of imported raw materials is subject to these and other conditions. The greater distance presents transport difficulties, which may be problems of loading, uncertain deliveries, complete stoppages in wartime (for example the cotton famine of 1862–5 caused by the American Civil War) and interference by governments in the form of duties and quotas. (The government of an importing country may limit the import of a particular item to a fixed volume in any one year, which is called a quota. This may be done to encourage production of the commodity within the country, to avoid importing more than can be paid for, or for other reasons.) These problems have often made the use of imported raw materials unattractive or impossible, even though plentiful supplies were available.

Manufacturing is affected by other factors as well. The demand for goods from within the country depends to a great extent on the purchasing power of the community, and of the different sections within the community. Woollen cloth requirements in the Middle Ages varied with the size of the population and with how often individuals could afford to buy new clothes. The wealthy could do this more often than others but alternating war and peace and the uncertainties of the harvest meant that their ability to purchase was constantly changing. So was their interest in woollen cloth, for the fashion industry is nothing new. The first calls on anyone's income are food and somewhere to live. As a person's income rises above these basic needs, the surplus becomes available for manufactured goods. Income levels and food prices therefore have a direct bearing on the volume of manufactured goods that the community can afford and directly affect the level of production.

Demands for goods also come from other communities. The Roman Conquest brought in its wake many traders buying for customers elsewhere in the Empire. This encouraged more people to manufacture goods for export. The creation of an empire in the eighteenth and nineteenth centuries formed a market much larger than the native population, and the colonies were required to buy their goods from the mother country. The level of spending by the colonies fluctuated in much the same way as it did in Britain, and manufacturers had to keep pace. Fluctuations in trade settled into a distinct pattern which can be clearly traced in the nineteenth century. The pattern is known as the trade cycle, which has a slow build up to a boom in trade, followed by a sudden slump, which slowly gives way to the growth of trade once more.

Other factors enter into the level of production. The quality of goods is clearly important. Poor quality goods will only sell if no others exist or if the others are very much more expensive. Good quality products, on the other hand, will sell both at home and abroad. The same applies to originality—goods will sell well if nothing similar is available, as was the case with the steam engines made by Boulton and Watt. Good quality and originality came together in the middle years of the nineteenth century when many British industries were better equipped and more imaginative than most other countries. Britain was called 'the workshop of the world' as a result, and its industries prospered until those of other countries took over the lead.

The level of technology within the country also has a direct bearing on the volume of industrial production. This varies too. It can be affected, for example, by how easy or difficult it is for a person to learn a skill, on how free he is to find work where he can use this skill and whether there are facilities for him to learn further skills. Another variable is the degree of inventiveness present in the country at any particular time. This can often be encouraged by the need to find a faster way of doing part of a process to allow production to be increased. Encouraging inventiveness (ie research) is a relatively new idea in industry, and formerly inventions arose spontaneously in response to a pressing need. This process was very marked in the eighteenth century. Inventions are of little use, however, unless they are utilised, and this requires sums of capital to be available to finance the construction of machinery until such time as it pays for itself. Few inventions will be used when they become available unless industrialists both have the money (or can borrow it cheaply) and see some advantage in adopting the new idea.

With so many variables affecting the level of industrial activity, it is clear that the story of industries in the past two thousand years will not be one of smooth and continuous development. Instead, most industries have developed at their own speeds, occasionally acting in harmony with others. While some industries expanded, others declined and many stood still. This is even more true of individual firms within industries. Several industries had been well established in prehistoric times but it is with the more detailed records of Roman times that this book begins.

SECTION A

ROMAN BRITAIN

2 Britain and the Romans

The Roman legions did not bring industry to Britain when Claudius led them across the Channel in 43. (All dates are AD unless BC is stated.) Many industries had flourished in Britain for several centuries, both to supply the needs of the natives and to provide a surplus for trade with other parts of Europe and even beyond. Phoenician boats had been buying tin from Cornwall for centuries; indeed tin was called the 'British metal' in Mediterranean countries, and had been mined for 2,000 years before Julius Caesar made his raids in 55 and 54 BC. The production of cloth and the manufacture of tools for agriculture and fishing are examples of the industries active when the Romans came. Imperial officials knew this beforehand for they had encouraged trade between the Empire and Britain.

One of the main incentives to conquer the island was to acquire greater control of this trade, and so tailor it more exactly to Roman needs. Conquest of Britain would give control of production to some extent, and at the least would give opportunities to expand the production of what might be called strategic materials, such as silver and copper. There were other reasons for the conquest apart from trade, of course, including the desire to stop the activities of pirates and raiders based in Britain which caused great disruption, particularly in Gaul (France). Control of production and trade must have been at least as important to Roman minds, since they normally conquered only those countries that could contribute something to the Empire. While in some colonies this was a plentiful supply of slaves or fighting men, in Britain the variety of minerals and manufactured goods would seem a more likely prize.

At this point it may be necessary to give a warning about interpreting words like 'industry' and 'trade' in a twentieth century way. Estimates of the population of Britain in 43 can be little more than speculation but a total of a million for the whole country is probably a generous estimate. Most of the country was still heavily wooded and the bears and wolves of legend roamed at liberty. The larger settlements were in the main river valleys of the South of England, such as the Thames and Severn valleys, where the climate and soil made farming a tolerable occupation. The largest settlements were no more than villages from a twentieth century viewpoint, and there were few of them. The country was inhabited by many tribes who made war on each other as occasion offered. Even the smallest villages were therefore defended by ditches and banks topped by palisades. Trade between neighbouring villages and tribes took place whenever peace permitted, which was probably more often than not. Difficulties of transport through a country full of wild animals, the natural hazards of marsh and flooded rivers and the unfailing displeasure of the weather made trading an event rather than a normality. More than a thousand years after the Romans had left, travelling traders were greeted in most parts of Britain with pleasure and surprise because of their rarity. Although traders in Roman times sometimes came from distant parts of Europe, even one from the next village must have made a welcome change.

Each settlement had therefore to be basically independent and any goods obtained through trade were luxuries; they might be quite ordinary objects for use in agriculture, yet their supply and replacement could not be relied upon. Such unexpected goods must be regarded as luxuries. Trade at this time was therefore an activity that affected most settlements very little. The exceptions were the larger settlements in the South, especially those on rivers or near the sea. Transport for them was easier, and they were closer to continental routes. Traders were a more common sight in such areas, and the goods far more varied than the other parts of England ever saw. There is no doubt that these southern settlements were richer.

Clearly the modern concept of a combine employing hundreds of people at many sites is wildly out of place. The mental picture of large and specialised factories has also to be forgotten. The pattern that the Romans found is harder to imagine. The extraction industries, mining for metals and stone, were probably the nearest to twentieth century practices. Nowadays a miner is a specialised worker who has often undergone extensive training. The miners of Roman times were also skilled workmen; it took years of experience to be able to recognise the ores of the metals among the other rocks, and to be able to guess which way to dig to follow a vein of ore. The bigger mines, such as the Cornish tin mines, also required the other mining skills, of being able to shore up rock walls and prop ceilings. There was, however, one great and complete difference between the miners in Roman times and now. It was quite impossible to allow large numbers from a settlement to specialise in mining, or anything else. The main concern of every family and village was to have sufficient food. Arable farming took up all the spring and summer months, and part of the others also, while the keeping of animals, or hunting and fishing, took up yet more time. Only when these demands had been met was it possible to consider another occupation, which had to be very much a part-time job. The nearest equivalent to this pattern in our own day is the custom of free-mining in the Forest of Dean in Gloucestershire; men who fulfil the necessary requirements of birth and residence can apply to open their own coal mine in the forest, which is a coalfield that was in use before Roman times. To this day the mining is a part-time activity, combined perhaps with keeping sheep, an inn, or a petrol station. The coal mining is a secondary occupation. The amounts of coal produced by these methods is slight, even with the use of modern tools and winding gear. It may reasonably be inferred that the quantities raised 2,000 years ago were even less, that they were normally only sufficient for modest local needs and that only occasionally did they provide an exportable surplus.

The manufacturing industries were even less like their twentieth century descendants. Some of them required highly skilled craftsmen, as in the processing of metals. Some needed workshops with special facilities, such as a potter needing a plentiful supply of water and space for kilns. Few villages, however, needed the full-time work of such men, and they took their part in farming along with the others, especially at the busier times of seedtime and harvest. The 'workshop' was normally part of the craftsman's own hut, though anything involving fire, as a kiln or forge, might well be put a safe distance away. The manufacture of cloth involved the whole family. The method of manufacturing goods in a person's home has been named the domestic system, or domestic manufacture, and will recur frequently in this book. In the bleaker parts of the country, where farming took a proportionately larger amount of time, many settlements had to rely entirely on what could be made at home, and had not even the luxury of the services of skilled craftsmen. Life and work was much more difficult.

Both life and work had been carried on in these ways for centuries, and continued in the same way for centuries more. Some parts of Britain were quite untouched by the Roman Conquest, or touched only occasionally, and in all areas the daily needs of the native population had to be met whether the Romans came or not. Roman engineers and administrators introduced some new ideas and methods and the ready sale of certain kinds of British goods, such as jet jewellery, stimulated several industries. The Roman view of their contribution to industrial development in Britain naturally takes up the brief mentions of such matters in Roman writings. But more in spite of the Conquest than because of it, the industries that had been in operation before 43 continued to produce goods to meet British needs. The surplus available for export was in some cases increased by Roman methods (the use of slave labour, for example, and some civil engineering projects), and the supply of metals was taken over entirely by Roman officials. The Conquest thus had a mixed influence upon the existing industries—some came under government control, others were encouraged by having wealthy colonists as customers (both privately and as traders), while in many areas industries continued to provide the goods wanted locally, regardless of the presence of Romans in the country.

The longer the occupation lasted (the remaining garrison troops were recalled in 410) the more trade was encouraged. Increasingly, there were long spells of peace over large parts of the country. In the northern counties, to take one example, there were no serious uprisings or invasions from 150 to 190, 200 to 290 and 300 to 350. These were long spans of time, and the intervening troubles were not so devastating as to discourage traders completely. Trade therefore increased, and the output of manufacturers had also to increase. The network of roads, mostly built in the first century, also assisted trade between settlements which had access to them. About 5,000 miles of road were constructed; most of this was for defence and administration, though some of the roads built in the third and fourth centuries were built solely for trade. Naturally, the bulk of trade along these roads was for Roman needs, such as the wheat and iron carried on Stane Street across the Weald to London. The roads could also serve local traders, especially those who sold their wares to garrisons and in the busy administrative towns. The roads, however, had been planned for troop movements to quell uprisings, and seldom went near the principal mining areas that would most have benefited from improved transport. Large areas lay far from these roads, making the movement of materials and even the learning of technological processes difficult or impossible.

3   Mines and Metals

The Romans put all metals under imperial control, just as soon as each mining area was conquered. The richest lead mines in Britain were in the Mendip hills in Somerset. The area was conquered and the mines reopened in 49, an indication of the importance attached to lead mining by the conquerors. The mines were under the control of resident officials, who used Charterhouse as their head office. These officials arranged for plentiful supplies of convicts and prisoners of war to do the mining, controlled the extent of mining, and stamped each pig of lead before forwarding it to customs officials at the ports—Southampton in the case of the Mendip mines. (The Romans were terrified of travel by sea and reduced all crossings to the minimum.) The great interest in lead was partly due to the quantities of it used in construction and domestic ware, but far more to the fact that the main type of lead ore found in Britain—galena—also contained silver. This was as valuable then as now, and was the basis of the imperial currency. Other mines were re-opened as soon as the resident tribes had been pacified: Flintshire in 74, Nidderdale in 81, soon followed by mines in the Swale and Wharfe dales, and others in Derbyshire, Shropshire and elsewhere.

The Romans were able to expand lead production for a while by the use of forced labour but it could not go on indefinitely. Miners were skilled men, and no matter how skilled the Roman officials might be there was no substitute for local knowledge and initiative. The Romans evidently thought the same, and handed the mines back to local individuals at intervals during the second century. The Yorkshire mines were relinquished after a revolt in

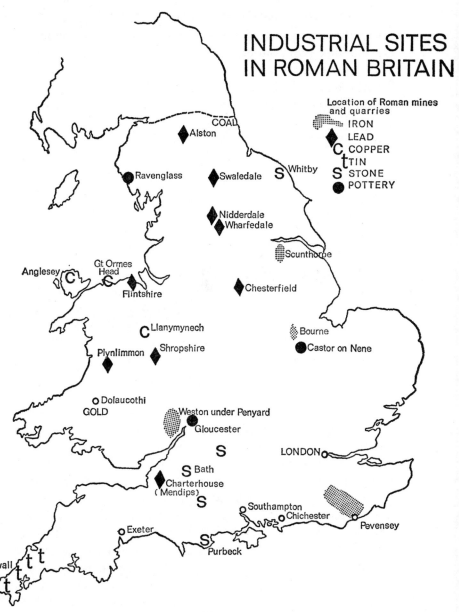

INDUSTRIAL SITES IN ROMAN BRITAIN

Location of Roman mines and quarries

- IRON
- ◆ LEAD
- C COPPER
- t TIN
- S STONE
- ● POTTERY

COAL

◆ Alston

● Ravenglass

◆ Swaledale

S Whitby

◆ Nidderdale
◆ Wharfedale

Scunthorpe

Anglesey C

Gt Ormes Head

C

◆ Flintshire

◆ Chesterfield

C Llanymynech

Bourne

◆ Plynlimmon

◆ Shropshire

● Castor on Nene

O Dolaucothi
GOLD

Weston under Penyard
● Gloucester

LONDON O

S

S Bath
◆ Charterhouse
(Mendips)

S

O Southampton
O Chichester

Pevensey

O Exeter

S

Purbeck

nwall t t t
t

Fig 1

154, while the Derbyshire mines came under the control of a group known as the Lutudarum company. The metal still remained the property of the state, even when some local people made some profit out of mining it. The legions ran their mines for their own needs in a few areas, such as at Alston in Northumberland and on the east slopes of Plynlimmon, Cardigan. These may have been new mines but it is more likely that, as in the other areas, the troops were simply taking over existing mines and developing them to produce more.

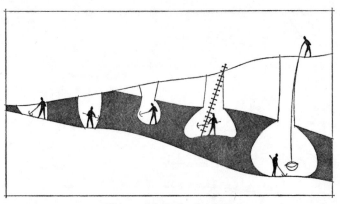

Fig 2 *Methods of mining*

Lead mining was usually open cast, that is the mine workings were open to the sky (Fig 2). Much of the lead worked at this time was either on the surface or close to it. Many mines were no more than shallow pits ten or twenty feet deep. The ore could be shovelled straight out of such holes until increasing depth made it necessary for the spoil to be carried up ladders in rush baskets. As the ore accessible in one pit was worked out another was begun further along the vein. Veins usually run in straight lines making them easy to follow. Deeper veins were mined by bell pits—a narrow shaft was dug until the ore was reached and this was extracted from as large an area at the foot of the shaft as it was safe to undercut. The cross-section of such a pit was similar to that of a bell. These pits seldom exceeded thirty feet in depth because of the dangers of flooding, lack of fresh air and collapse of the shaft.

Galena is heavy, so the smelting was done as near the pits as possible. The rock was hammered down to the size of gravel and the galena sorted from the waste rock. Both jobs were probably done by hand. The ore was then ready for smelting, that is heating it to separate the lead from the impurities that combine with it to form galena. The main impurity was sulphur, which readily combined with the carbon in the brushwood or peat normally used as fuel. The smelting furnace was normally little more than a pile of stones built to form a basin (Fig 3). This was erected

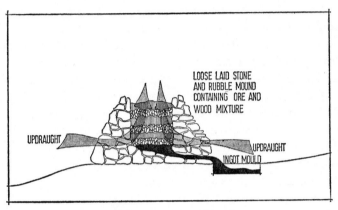

Fig 3 *Diagram of a smelting furnace*

where it would catch the wind, to keep the fire burning well. Ore was thrown on when the fire was well alight. More fuel was added if the fire began to fade and more ore if things went well. In this way a continuous sandwich of fuel and ore could be made, until the pool of molten lead grew too large. One side of the furnace was then breached and the lead allowed to run out into a long, narrow hole in the ground, where it solidified. The block of lead, called a pig, was dug out and stamped with the official details and sent on its way to Rome. Pigs of lead weighed about a hundred pounds and were sent by water wherever possible. Pigs from the Chesterfield mines went via quite small streams to the Humber and were put aboard ship in Hull. The movements of lead were extensive under the Romans, as has been shown by the seventy pigs found in all parts of Britain that were first lost between mine and port. Officials at the ports decided where the lead should go. Some of it was needed by the legions, yet more was used in constructing buildings. The rest was despatched to Rome.

Some of the lead retained in Britain was kept to extract the silver. This was a long and difficult process. The amount of silver in a ton of lead is very slight—twenty or thirty ounces would be normal. The first necessity in recovering the silver was to concentrate the silver in a smaller amount of lead. The lead was melted and allowed to crystallise. Almost pure lead crystallised first and could be separated from the rest. This process was repeated until the silver content rose to one or two per cent. The lead (strictly, lead-silver alloy) was then placed in a cupellation furnace. The cupel was a shallow, saucer-like container that could be heated from below. Air was blown over the surface of the molten lead, which oxidised it to a powder and blew it away, leaving the silver in the cupel. These methods were not very efficient, and the slag-heaps in the Mendips have been worked and re-worked as better methods have been devised. However, the Romans' need for silver made complex and wasteful methods worthwhile.

GOLD

Gold was worked at only one site in Britain: Dolau Cothi near Llandovery in Carmarthenshire. Mining seems to have been carried on there for some time before the arrival of the Romans, but they developed the mines dramatically after their conquest of the area in about 75. Rock was brought down in the open-cast mines there in the second and third centuries by undercutting it (see Fig 4). The pit props were burnt away and the rock left to fall. Water was used to move the fallen debris, and for other purposes. Two aqueducts were built to bring water from streams further up in the hills. These aqueducts were four and seven miles long, and the water was held in great storage tanks. It could be released from these as a controlled flood down the hillside to wash away soil when prospecting for new places to mine, and to move waste rock. The use of water in this way was called hushing. Galleries were tunnelled into the hillside in places where

26

open-cast mining was unsuitable. In these, the rock was dug either with hammers and gads (wedges) or by fire-setting—heating up the rock and then cooling it quickly with cold water, causing it to contract and splinter.

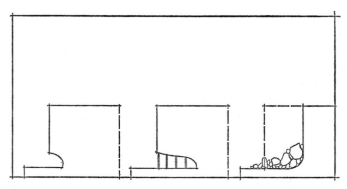

Fig 4 *Process of undercutting rock to bring down a quarry face*

However the rock was brought down, it was then crushed to the consistency of gravel, probably by nothing more ambitious than many men with hammers. A number of querns from grindstones have been found on the site, which suggests that the gravel was further reduced to a fine dust by grinding it again by hand. Using water to sort the dust, gold sank to the bottom first in a settling tank because of its weight and the rock dust sank on top. Once the tank had been drained, the rock fragments were shovelled away, leaving the gold dust.

Another possibility that has been put forward is that the stream of water containing grains of gold was passed over or through a sheep's fleece at such a speed that the heavier gold was able to sink into the fleece while everything else was swept on. Roman metallurgists discovered that gold could also be regained from crushed rock by dissolving it out in mercury and distilling the mercury from the solution to leave the gold behind. Gold and silver were also recovered from copper.

All the methods of obtaining the gold were difficult and expensive and the quantities produced in Wales were unlikely to have been very great. Gold has always been scarce and valuable, however, and was reckoned worth the trouble. The greatest cost was in the efforts and lives of the slaves used for this work, but the Romans took no account of them. The bulk of the gold undoubtedly went to Rome as part of the taxes to be paid by the colony.

TIN AND COPPER

Tin had been mined in Cornwall before the Romans came and widely exported. The Romans took little notice of these mines at first. They were never brought under imperial control as Cornwall was never conquered by the Romans. This was no great loss as the Romans had plentiful supplies of tin from Spanish mines. These and their other sources of supply gave out about the middle of the third century, giving them a new interest in the Cornish mines. These were now kept busy and expanded, the miners apparently selling the ingots of smelted tin to the Romans. The mines were shallow shaft mines with galleries opening out from the shafts following the elusive veins of ore. The ore was crushed on the surface and smelted with charcoal or, more probably, peat.

Tin was valued by the Romans because of the alloys that could be made from it. A popular metal was pewter, made of 30 per cent lead and 70 per cent tin. This was used to make tableware, such as plates and flagons, all of which polished up well. Blocks of pewter were exported to Rome. Much more tin was alloyed with copper to make bronze, a metal with both ornamental and practical uses.

The copper for bronze was normally obtained from a rich supply in Spain but mines were developed in Britain from the third century. The principal mines under Roman control were at Great Orme's Head in Caernarvonshire and at Llanymynech in Shropshire, both of which were mined in the third and fourth centuries. Adit mining was used at Great Orme's Head. A gallery was dug into the hillside, rising a little above horizontal so as to be self-draining. Side galleries could be cut to drain into the main adit. At Llanymynech a large cave was extended with galleries, the miners sleeping in the cave. Convicts and slaves were again the workers. The crushing and smelting were done by private companies.

A richer source of supply was the island of Anglesey, head-quarters of the Druids. The copper was mined by freemen in Parys Mountain and smelted in the villages. The Druids had to send the smelted blocks as tribute, a payment for not being conquered. Some idea of the importance the Romans attached to these sources of supply was shown in the last fifty years of the occupation. Although Chester was abandoned in 367, a garrison was kept in Caernarvon for a further sixteen years—the copper mines were well worth guarding from pirates, and the skilled workers from slave-raiders. Some of the copper was used in Britain, both as copper and in bronze, and the rest despatched to Rome.

IRON

The iron produced under Roman control was probably all used in Britain and most of it for military purposes. (Some had been exported before the Conquest and this trade may have continued in part.) The conquerors took over the mines in the Weald of Sussex almost as soon as they landed and mines in the Forest of Dean were captured in 74–6. Mines were later opened up in Northamptonshire, Lincolnshire and in a few other places, though the Weald and Forest of Dean remained the most important areas, production from the latter increasing steadily throughout the occupation. The mines were almost always bell pits and employed few men.

The smelting of iron required much greater heat than lead. Blast furnaces had therefore to be built of stone. These were cylindrical, open at the top and had holes near the bottom to allow the air in to keep the fire hot. The wind could be augmented with bellows. Charcoal was the fuel and was readily available from the forests surrounding the mines. Unlike lead, the iron did not melt when the impurities were burnt away. The furnace was broken open when a sufficient amount of ore had been smelted. In the middle of all the rock and fuel fragments was a spongy lump of iron called a bloom, so the smelting furnace became known as a bloomery. The bloom was taken out and hammered while still red-hot, to beat out remaining slag. The iron was reheated if necessary and hammered until as many of the impurities as possible were removed. The heating and hammering also made the iron harder and less brittle, and it was then called wrought iron. The blocks of iron were sent off to the nearest centre of iron forging, which was Chichester for the Weald and Weston-under-Penyard in Gloucestershire.

COAL

The Romans had only slight interest in coal, using it only when wood and charcoal were not available. It is very unlikely that the British had any use for coal at all, except possibly where it outcropped on the surface. Coal was never carried far from the mines, though a strange exception to this was that wheat ships returning to the fens from Newcastle were ballasted with coal, which was mostly dumped in the sea at the journey's end.

Mining was entirely by shallow holes and bell pits—the uses that could be found for coal did not justify anything ambitious. Bell pits were found during excavations at Benwell on Hadrian's Wall, which suggests that the troops could warm themselves by open braziers while on guard duty. These pits were between twelve and fifteen feet deep. Further along the Wall, at Housesteads, a guardroom was found full of coal, and a cobbler situated outside the fort had a bunkerful. Excavations in many parts of Britain have given evidence of the use of coal for central heating in Wroxeter and Caerwent, and for cooking in Manchester and South Shields. A third-century book, *Collection of Memorable Facts*, mentions the use of coal to keep the altar flame burning in Bath. Industrially, coal was used to smelt lead in Pentre Ffwrndau and to melt (not smelt) iron and glass in Wilderspool. (It is interesting but not necessarily conclusive that the evidence of the use of coal has mostly come from Roman sites.) There were coal mines in Somerset, Nottinghamshire, Lancashire and Newcastle upon Tyne, and possibly in other areas where the coal was near the surface. However, coal was only used for convenience—nobody was interested in taking it any distance when wood, charcoal and peat were available in most parts of Britain and far easier to handle and transport than coal.

The common kind of hut built by the British was circular. A wall 2–3ft high served as foundation for poles which both supported the thatched roof and anchored the wattle and daub of the walls. The stones for the wall often came from cleaning the fields and were not specially quarried. Even the large flat stones put in doorways to minimise wear could often be found near at hand.

The Romans frequently used timber in building forts, and large quantities of stone were only needed in the towns and later for country villas. Stone is bulky and almost valueless, so the Roman architects made do with local materials wherever possible. It may be imagined that slaves and convicts were again drafted to the nearest hillside that would yield usable stone. The quarries made by such digging were small and soon abandoned.

Larger and more permanent quarries were opened in two areas. One of these was Bath in Somerset, where the creamy limestone was much admired and quarried from 61. The baths in Bath were built of this stone, and a visit to them gives a clear idea of what Roman architects could do with good materials. Despite all the difficulties of transport this stone was used on the other side of the Severn at Lydney, also in London and even further afield. In these more remote areas the stone was usually used for ornament or for capping walls. It says something for Roman determination and architectural taste that they were prepared to move stone bodily round the country, though the cost in British lives may well have been considerable.

The other main stone quarry was on the Isle of Purbeck in Dorset. A kind of marble was quarried there which, though not as fine as Italian marble was good enough for domestic purposes, monumental panels and the like, while Italian marble was imported for temples and other public buildings. Shale was also quarried and was put to many uses. The best shale was fine grained and came in several colours. It could be split into thin flat sheets and panels. It was used decoratively to panel walls, and even trays and plates were made from it. It was also used in jewellery (See below, p 39.)

Vast quantities of stone were used in constructing the 5,000 miles of road that the Romans built. Minor roads were 16ft wide, main roads 24ft wide, and the depth could be 2ft or more. There could be no thought of transporting such quantities any distance, so quarries were opened up at intervals along the line of the road. The foundations of these roads varied with the geology of the area. Loose gravel was preferred for the surface and could be carried some way over partly made roads. The engineer would not insist on it if it was not readily available but would turn to a local alternative such as the iron slag used in the Forest of Dean, which rusted into a very hard-wearing surface. The quarrying of stone for the roads must have employed large numbers, especially in the period of most rapid construction from 43 to 81, but the quarries were small and scattered. They have left few traces of their existence. Perhaps the roads themselves are adequate memorials of those who built them. The craftsmen who manufactured goods from the mined minerals have also left many examples of their work, which must next be considered.

PLACES TO VISIT

Much of the aqueducts and storage tanks remain at Dolau Cothi, Pumpsaint, Carmarthen. Roman roads may be seen near Goathland on the North Yorkshire Moors and at Blackpool Bridge in the Forest of Dean in Gloucestershire, and a bridge at Castle Combe, Wiltshire. Site museums have been set up after most major excavations, and contain many examples of industrial activity. Much of the baths exist at Bath, Somerset. See also the list of museums at the end of the book.

Page 33 (above) The foundation and kerb stones of the Roman road from Mitcheldean to Lydney, Gloucestershire, which can be seen at Blackpool Bridge; (below) a hand-loom weaver busy in the fifteenth century. A shuttle is passed from hand to hand in the shed—the space made by raising half the warp threads and lowering the others, which is done by the treadles. The width of the cloth is limited by the reach of the weaver's arms.

Page 34 (*above*) Cloth was bought by merchants undyed, like the pieces behind this merchant. The cloth was boiled in a lead pan, and stirred by long stangs so that each piece was dyed evenly; (*below*) fulling was added to corn grinding, where both could be run from the same water wheel. This late eighteenth-century corn and fulling mill was developed on a medieval site.

4 Made in Britain

It is not easy to tell whether objects found in archaeological excavations were made in this country or imported. Roman officials came from other parts of the Empire, especially in the first century, and naturally had their own likes and dislikes. They may have continued to buy from abroad, or they may have found that British craftsmen were sufficiently skilled to be able to make the goods they required. Goods of lead and iron were certainly made in this country, though it is harder to say where gold and silver objects were made. It would seem that British craftsmen were certainly capable of producing most of the metal goods so far found in Britain, but that is not to say that they did so.

Gold and silver were largely used for money, as were copper, bronze and brass. (Brass was an alloy of copper and zinc carbonate, and was very difficult to make. It was as highly valued as silver at times.) Large amounts of currency were coined in Britain during the occupation. The first stage was to cast flat discs of metal in stone or clay moulds. Iron dies were prepared by having the design wanted on the finished coin cut in reverse on the end of the die. One die was fixed to something solid, a disc placed on the face and the other die was hammered on top. This often resulted in some strange shapes, which can be seen in museum collections.

Goldsmiths and silversmiths produced many kinds of tableware, though the customers for such goods could only be a handful of the highest paid officials. Plates, fruit bowls, drinking cups and wine ewers, and elaborate candelabra were made, adding distinction to any home. Temple statues were made of, or more usually coated with, gold and silver. Plates and bowls were made by hammering the metal into shape. Silver, gold, copper and bronze can be stretched a long way before they split, provided they are frequently heated and cooled to keep them workable. A skilled silversmith can start with a flat disc and, by hammering against a block of wood or a padded rest, shape it into a bowl; the process is called raising. Considerable ornamentation was incorporated, such as handles or a decorative rim. Complex goods such as ewers were assembled from several raised sections soldered together.

Bronze was used for similar goods and was also used to decorate furniture and other parts of the house and to make mirrors. Small objects were forged straight from a heated piece of metal, hammered into shape on an anvil. Objects such as door hinges could be made quite easily in this way. Larger items such as cauldrons were cast. A mould was made in clay or stone and molten bronze poured in. The mould was opened or knocked to pieces when the bronze was cool and the casting inspected. Any irregularities could be altered by heating the bronze and hammering the casting until it was right. Large items, such as statues, were made as a number of castings which could later be fitted together.

The finest bronze castings were made by a delicate method called the lost wax process. Small figures of people or animals were the kinds of object made in this way. A clay model was made of the animal, a dog for example, which was coated with beeswax. The fine details of the dog's eyes, mouth, tongue and whiskers were carved in the wax—clay was too coarse for such details. The completed carving was covered in wet clay and ashes, which were put on almost liquid so that they followed the details in the wax. A thicker layer of clay was built up around it all and bronze rods pushed through to hold everything in place. The mould was baked in an oven, which both hardened the clay and melted out the wax, and molten bronze was poured into the space left. The finished casting had all the features carved in the wax and the clay core was chipped out to leave the casting hollow. A final polishing finished the dog, as all bronze goods had to be carefully polished.

Pewter was also highly polished. All kinds of tableware were made from it. Most goods were made by raising, and the metal was relatively easy to work because of the high lead content which made the metal soft. It was cheaper by far than the other metals, and pewter objects were bought by many more officials and army officers than could afford bronze.

The workmen in all these metals had workshops, though they were commonly one-man workshops. Tongs and hammers made up most of the tools needed, together with a forge or furnace for the metals that needed constant heating. A single room cabin must have been adequate for many craftsmen, perhaps little different from the workshops of the serpentine workers on the Lizard in Cornwall in our own day.

The manufacture of lead goods was doubtless done in similar surroundings. The metal was put to all manner of uses. Gutters, drainpipes, roofing material, for water pipes, sinks, basins, water pumps—the list is endless. Lead sheet could be made quite easily and it was then straightforward to fold it around a mould and solder the join to make pipes of any required size and shape.

Iron was quite another matter. Some iron was exported from the smelting furnaces in the Weald and Gloucestershire; much was put to use in Britain. Weston-under-Penyard was the centre of iron working in the Forest of Dean and Chichester in the Weald. Blacksmiths in both towns were kept busy producing tools and military goods of all kinds. The flat broadsword carried by all Roman legions was made of iron. Their nine foot spear was made in such a way as to be used once only: some were made half of iron and half of wood so that they broke on impact, others had the iron softened behind the tip so that they bent against whatever they struck. Six pound darts to be fired from catapults were tipped with iron. Troops wore a cuirass, which was made of plates of iron jointed together with loose strips covering any places where gaps might appear. Quite apart from weapons, troops also carried picks and shovels to enable them to construct their square camps and forts at speed.

All this represented considerable work for the blacksmith, as did his own need for anvils, tongs, frame saws, files, wire-drawing dies, hammers, cold chisels and so forth. The legions had their own blacksmiths (there was a military workshop at Corbridge, making weapons and nails) but much of the work must have been done by native British workmen. Since the people overrun by the Romans are often described as living in the Iron Age and iron was smelted in Britain from c 650 BC, there can have been no shortage of such skilled men. The British tribes used iron swords and iron-tipped spears. They also had uses for iron in farming, for picks, hoes and parts of ploughs. The Romans brought a reaping machine into Britain which used iron for the cutting bar and for strapping to hold it together. They do not seem to have used iron in building in Britain, though it was used to bind and reinforce buildings in some parts of the Empire.

All these goods were made from wrought iron, that is the iron was heated up in a forge to red heat and hammered to shape on an anvil. This was even true of the large cauldrons used for steeping meat. The high temperatures needed to melt iron were not possible (except for very small quantities) without large blast furnaces and these do not seem to have come to Britain until much later. It was possible to weld two pieces of iron together by making them white hot and hammering them together. This process was used on occasions to give a sword better cutting edges. The body of the sword blade was made of iron and the extra strips welded on were made of iron heated in a charcoal furnace, which had made it into blister steel. Iron was also riveted, both to other pieces of iron and to other metals.

In this survey of manufacturing methods used 2,000 years ago, all the main methods of metal working have been seen to be used. Metals could be cast, forged, soldered, riveted and welded—almost all the methods now used. Using these methods the craftsmen of the time could produce a wide range of articles, ranging from utilitarian nails to objects of beauty.

JEWELLERY

The Romans and Britons were alike in the pleasure they derived from jewellery, and men wore as much as women. These remarks have immediately to be qualified by adding that jewellery was expensive and could by no means be afforded by all.

The objects made of gold and silver and the alloy of those,

called electrum, were the most expensive, partly because these were the rare metals and partly because for that reason more elaborate methods were used. Attractive patterns were made by cutting very thin strips and interlacing them. This is called filigree work. Other effects were made by soldering tiny globules of the metals to a base, a process known as granulation. Other designs were obtained by inlaying strips of one metal into another, and by raising patterns or pictures in relief by hammering from the reverse side (*repoussé* work). Hand-worked jewellery found near the Dolau Cothi gold mine suggest the industry was carried on there.

Bronze was also used widely for jewellery and for ornamental clasps and buckles for togas and cloaks. British craftsmen had been making all manner of bronze objects long before the arrival of the Romans. They were fond of making dragon shapes, among others, and were very skilled in overlaying the metal with enamels of bright colours.

Jewellery was also made from stones of many kinds and values. Amethyst was popular at the expensive end of the range (and so were pearls found in rivers, especially the Scottish Dee). Shale has been mentioned before, being mined in the Isle of Purbeck. The stone was turned on a lathe to form bracelets and bangles. The most popular stone with the Romans was jet. This came from the east coast of Yorkshire and was made into hairpins and spindles, and also rings, pendants, bracelets and necklaces. Medallions were carefully carved with family groups and the Romans also had a craze for teddy bears on them. The stone was lightly burnished, unlike the jet used in Victorian times which was highly polished.

POTTERY AND GLASS

The best known variety of Roman pottery is the red Samian ware, which was imported. Much pottery was made in Britain and the Romans influenced design considerably. Earthenware goods such as bowls and storage jars had been made in Britain for some time with various kinds of decoration. These goods were made on a potter's wheel and fired in a kiln. The Romans brought new ways of preparing the clay, leading to thinner pottery. They also added new styles of ornament, having a particular preference for moulded scenes and slip decoration (which was dipping the pot in liquid clay that had been coloured).

There were a number of quite large potteries, operating over long periods whose goods are found over a large area. One of these was at work in the New Forest in the third and fourth centuries, and supplied goods to much of southern England. Its range of products was impressive—flagons, dishes, table and kitchen bowls, jars, cooking pots, vases, goblets, cups and candlesticks, all in different designs. Many items were decorated with scrolls or triangles in white slip, others were stamped with rosettes. The Midlands and much of the North of England was supplied with goods from a pottery at Caister-on-Nene, which specialised in making drinking cups. These were decorated with hunting scenes, chariot races, gladiators and ivy leaves, which were applied both by moulding and barbotine (which is similar to piping icing sugar on a cake). This pottery was at work from the second to the fourth century.

These factories were long lasting and large; there were many more, serving local needs, which came and went. Clay was dug at Grimescar near Huddersfield and made into tiles, pipes and coarse pottery, none of which travelled very far from the area, and there were large numbers of such local works. The legions ran their own tile works in some places, as at Silchester and Gloucester. Roman villas and permanent barracks used large quantities of tiles for roofs and floors, as well as square section pipes for heating rooms. These requirements were so novel that they had to make the goods themselves until British workers learned how to copy them. Private makers of tiles in Gloucester had a thriving trade with the main camp there and the many villas being built in the Cotswolds.

The manufacture of glass, by contrast, was seldom done in Britain at this time. Glass jars and bottles were used, most glass goods being imported from the Rhineland. The only glass made in this country was of a very ordinary quality, being made by heating a mixture of soda, lime and sand to 1,000° C in a charcoal kiln. Small amounts of copper tinted the glass blue-green, while iron made it green-brown. Small objects were moulded, and glass blowing was introduced in the first century. Malton in Yorkshire was one of the centres for glass production.

TEXTILES

A shower-resistant cloak made of goats' wool was exported from Britain in the third century, a garment that must have been well tried by troops serving on Hadrian's Wall. Very fine linen was made in Yorkshire and was also well known. The Druids' white robes were probably linen that had been bleached, and linen was worn by wealthy Romans and their priests. It was also used for sheets, table cloths and napkins, and bath towels. The main kind of fabric made, however, was woollen cloth. Sheep abounded in Britain and the climate demanded a warm cloth. It had been made in this country for a long time and Julius Caesar first saw tartans in Britain, where they were used for cloaks.

The many processes required to make cloth are explained at greater length in the following chapter and it will be necessary here only to summarise the methods and note the differences. The cleaned wool was spun on a drop spindle, a slow process still in use in the Middle Ages. Weaving was done on a warp-weighted loom (Fig 5), which was little more than a square frame fixed in the ground or leant against a wall. The warp threads (doubled for strength) were arranged vertically and the weaving was done from the top down. The warp threads were gathered into bundles near the ground and weighted with stones or pottery weights to keep the tension constant. When finished the cloth was washed and much of it may have been used like that. Better cloths were dyed, fulled (making them stronger and warmer), and then cropped with shears.

The Romans brought new ideas into making cloth in the third century. A number of old villas were available at this time and they were taken over to house the finishing processes. Fulling (felting the cloth) was carried on extensively in a villa at Chedworth in the Cotswolds, and the cropping of fulled cloth in another at Great Chesterford near Cambridge. A dye works was set up at Silchester. A weaving factory was set up in Winchester to supply cloth to the forces, and it seems that most of the processes were concentrated in one group of buildings. However, while the encouragement and the new methods undoubtedly produced cloth in the quantities required by the Romans it is unlikely that the new ways had much impact on either the manufacturers or fashions of the British tribes. Changes did come about in the woollen industry in the thousand years after the Romans left but the changes came mostly towards the end of that time. In this industry, as in nearly all those that have been discussed in this section, the influence of the Roman occupation did not long outlast its collapse. In part this was due to the fact that the industries had been in existence for some time before the Romans came, so that the changes they introduced were intended either to increase the supply of goods to pay the taxes or to satisfy the demand for luxury goods. When the customers and customs officials left, most industries seem to have returned to producing for their own requirements as they had needed to during the occupation. The impending arrivals of Saxons, Picts and Vikings are likely to have caused far more serious changes to industries than the Roman occupation.

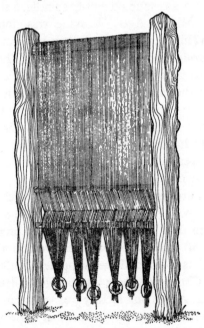

Fig 5   *Artist's impression of a warp-weighted loom*

Examples of Roman manufactured goods may be seen in many museums, including Aldborough Roman Museum, Yorkshire; the County Museum, Carmarthen; Pig Yard Museum, Settle; the Yorkshire Museum, York, and the museums set up on sites where excavations have taken place. There is also much to see at Chedworth Villa, Gloucester, and the Roman Palace, Fishbourne, Sussex.

SECTION B

450–1750

5 Developing Industries

The span of time covered by this section, 1,300 years, is very long. During this time the population slowly increased from an estimated one million in Roman times to about six million in 1750. This slow growth was accompanied by an equally slow increase in the volume of goods mined, manufactured and moved about the country. The increase was not only in quantity; the variety of goods available also widened over the centuries. This was made possible by steady advances in technical knowledge, brought about by a blend of native inventions and the experience of immigrants. Manufacturers were encouraged by the policies of the monarchy or of parliament, both of which frequently aimed at expanding trade with other countries. Through trade treaties and, from the seventeenth century, the slow acquisition of an empire, traders were given the chance to sell far more goods than they could ever have done in Britain alone. The increased trade made it worthwhile for manufacturers to build fulling mills in the fourteenth century, blast furnaces in the sixteenth, glass works in the seventeenth, and many other expensive structures throughout the period covered in this section.

Industrial development over these years was far from being even and continuous. The departure of the Roman garrisons in 410 was a disappointment only to those who relied on selling goods to the troops. They were not many, since the legions had their own blacksmiths, plumbers and other trades, and the disappointment mainly applied to people working in the luxury trades in the Roman towns. It is probable that trade between Britain and the Roman Empire continued at least for a while, and even more that the bulk of the population carried on their normal village activities as if nothing significant had happened. The tribal pattern had never really been broken even where tribes had become subservient to the Romans. Life in most villages had continued as before, except that they had had to pay the heavy taxes demanded by the occupying forces. Increased output or self-denial had been necessary to pay these taxes.

Most of the Roman towns were abandoned during the fifth century as the Britons returned to their hill-top defensive villages. The roads were also ignored over most of the country, since the system had little to do with where the communities lived. Short lengths came in useful but the traders mostly reverted to using the network of grass tracks that had emerged over the centuries.

The state of industry in Britain at this time is largely unknown. The period is often referred to as the Dark Ages, being shrouded in mystery. Few written records survive and archaeologists are only now beginning to piece a picture together. It would seem that the pattern of industry was much as it had been in the first century, with each village being as near self-sufficient as it could be. Building styles changed from the round hut to the long house, though construction was similar. The travelling trader still supplied those articles that could not be produced locally.

The threat to trade, and to life itself, came less from inter-tribal battles than from external raiders. Occasional raids by Angles, Saxons and Jutes had been made from the end of the third century and had been repulsed by joint Roman–British operations. The raids became colonising ventures from the fifth century, leading to the establishment of separate kingdoms in the east and south of England. The Britons could do no more than retreat to the hilly regions of the north, west and south-west. Neither they nor the new settlers were safe, for the Viking raiders caused frequent devastation before themselves settling in many parts of Britain. Indirectly the raids indicate that goods were still being manufactured. In addition to food and captives the raiders often took gold and silverware from churches, and cloth and money from the larger houses. While it is possible that church ornaments were imported, it is more likely in these troubled times that they were made somewhere in Britain. The goods taken by the raiders are an indication that some people in Britain

LOTHIAN

STRATHCLYDE

Areas of Norwegian settlements.

GALLOWAY

BERNICIA

CUMBRIA

NORSE KINGDOM OF YORK

GWYNEDD

DANISH MERCIA

Principality of RHODRI MAWR

ENGLISH MERCIA

GUTHRUM'S KINGDOM

DYFED

MORGANNWG

WESSEX

CORNWALL

THE PRINCIPAL KINGDOMS
IN BRITAIN c. 900

Fig 6

could afford to buy manufactured articles of beauty, and implies the ability of craftsmen to make those, and therefore more ordinary, objects. Excavations and chance finds confirm the picture.

Britain was a maze of separate kingdoms by the eighth century, each with its own currency and language. Some of these languages still exist: Gaelic is still spoken in Scotland and Welsh in Wales, while the Cornish language only died out in the eighteenth century. Some of the Saxon languages combined to form the basis of English, but local dialect words show that English was not always as it is now.

There were fewer major invasions in the eighth century and many regions enjoyed a period of relative peace and stability. This encouraged trade and allowed manufacturers to develop a little. British linen, to take one example, was highly regarded in north European countries where it was sold at this time, and there seem to have been improvements in wool cloth production and dyeing techniques.

Such developments were encouraged when Alfred, king of Wessex (849–901) brought a greater measure of political unity to central and southern England than at any time since the Romans had left. Alfred's purpose was mainly to combat the Danish invaders who had settled in eastern England, but it also served to encourage many industries, including shipbuilding. The high quality of enamelled jewellery made in the ninth century is some indication of the advantages of peace and stability.

After the Norman invasion of 1066 the greater part of England was speedily brought under Norman control. Their passion for castle and church building developed stone quarrying and building techniques and, later, glass production. Norman barons sought to develop their estates to the full, which meant that they both expanded the production of raw materials and had money enough to buy the manufactured goods. Some areas specialised in certain products from an early date, as, for example, the edge-tool makers in Sheffield.

Throughout all this time, and indeed the full 1,300 years of this section, agriculture was the dominant industry. Farming methods were only slightly above subsistence level and the bulk

Page 51   This early view of a glass works shows lime and sand being brought on foot, while the man in the centre shovels ashes left from a fire. The kiln and glass-blowing methods remained much the same for centuries. Note the lack of trees near the works which was in central Europe.

Page 52 This fifteenth-century drawing of the construction of Noah's ark shows the methods used by house builders of the time. There is a wide range of tools, and note the man on the right of the roof knocking in a wooden trenail to pin the joint.

Fig 7 *A sixteenth-century brick moulder, and the kiln beyond him*

of the population had to employ itself in growing food. The blacksmith, corn miller, wheelwright and others had to fit their work around the farming year. Only in the growing towns could silversmiths, tailors, lawyers and others work full-time at their trade, earning enough money to buy their food.

The four hundred years following the Conquest saw a slow rise in the population, occasionally reduced by outbreaks of plague. The most serious was the Black Death in 1348–9 which reduced the population by a third. There were also frequent wars, of which the most troublesome to industry were the civil wars of the Roses in the fifteenth century. The Tudor dynasty, beginning with Henry VII in 1485, appreciated the need for peace and set out to encourage trade. This was of particular benefit to the woollen industry early in the sixteenth century but also assisted other manufacturers and shipbuilders.

Fig 8   *A tanner at work*

The encouragement given to Flemish and French immigrants in the fourteenth and sixteenth centuries contributed greatly to technical knowledge. Those who settled in East Anglia brought the new draperies and expanded the local worsted industry beyond recognition. Others brought new methods in iron and brass processing, in paper production and printing and in glass making. All received some encouragement from the government and their knowledge led to a marked increase in the numbers of people working in industries, and in the range of products. The dissolution of the monasteries in the 1530s helped by making available large disused buildings, frequently with access to water power, and also dispersed the people skilled in those trades that had been carried on by the monasteries.

The development of industries continued steadily throughout the seventeenth and early eighteenth centuries, apart from during the Civil War in the 1640s. The great trading companies were active and brought new raw materials and found markets for manufactured goods. Profits from trade and land improvements were available for investment in machinery and factory buildings, enclosures of land freed people for full-time industrial work as well as making it possible to grow a surplus of food with which to feed them. The alternating pattern of war and peace stimulated different industries in turn, encouraging them to make use of new inventions. The roads were resurfaced by the turnpike trusts, while wagonways and river improvements eased the transport of bulky loads. With increasing speed, the country's industries were equipping themselves for a complete change from the one-man part-time workshops that had characterised the bulk of this period to the full-time specialist-worker factories that would become normal in the nineteenth century. The final factor in the long development of Britain as an industrial nation began about 1750 as an unprecedented and sustained growth of the population, as will be seen later. In summary, the development of industrialisation during this period may be seen as a slow process to the thirteenth century when several factors began a slight expansion of industrial activity. This expansion increased markedly in the sixteenth century, and the new levels of activity were maintained into the eighteenth century.

6 The Woolsack, and Other Yarns

The production of fibres and fabrics was far and away the most important group of industries during the whole of this period. A large part of the customs revenue in the Middle Ages was derived from the export of wool, and the manufacture of some kind of cloth was done in every county in Britain. The textile industry has always been subject to changes in fashions, as will be seen in this chapter, but throughout this period woollen and linen cloth were made in large quantities. In the tenth century, for example, linen was preferred in England for underclothes (wearing a woollen shirt next to the skin was used as a penance in monasteries) and wool for top clothes. For the purpose of clarity the various fabrics are treated separately in this chapter.

WOOL

The woollen industry was the only major industry in Britain up to 1750. Many people who were mainly employed in farming combined with this some part of woollen manufacture. The bulk of the population in the Middle Ages were clothed only in wool, such as the sombre habits of the monks and the gaudier jerkins and doublets of townsmen. While the woollen industry remained the only important one, there were many changes within it. Customers came to demand and manufacturers to supply higher quality goods, immigrants introduced new methods and new cloths to the country and some areas came to specialise in producing certain types of cloth, such as West Country broad cloths and Welsh flannel.

There were plentiful supplies of wool available within Britain in the early part of this period, as the country was well known for its sheep. The keeping of sheep was greatly extended by the monks, particularly by the Cistercians who came to England in the twelfth century. This order deliberately chose wild areas in which to start, such as the densely wooded Wye valley in Gloucestershire where the monastery was built at Tintern, or Fountains Abbey in Yorkshire. The monasteries were given generous areas of land by wealthy noblemen, since the monks were only seeking the waste lands which nobody was using. Fountains Abbey was estimated to own a million acres of Yorkshire by the end of the fifteenth century. The bulk of this was used for grazing sheep, and the wool was sold to overseas buyers to pay for the gracious buildings. Fountains sold 27,600lb (the fleece from one sheep weighed 1½lb) to merchants from Florence in 1315, and the total production would have been more than that. The Cistercians were joined in wool trading by the Augustinian, Gilbertine, Benedictine and other orders, especially by individual monasteries in Yorkshire, the West Midlands and the Cotswolds.

Monasteries were not the only suppliers of wool, for many of the wealthy landowners kept large flocks on the lands they retained. These men sold some of their wool to overseas buyers but also supplied much to be made into cloth in this country. The cloth manufacturers were well organised in craft gilds by 1164, and the main cloth towns were London and York, Lincoln, Winchester and Oxford. The export of raw wool was controlled by the Merchants of the Staple, formed in 1313. Soon after this time there was a pronounced increase in the amount of cloth produced in this country, a process that was encouraged by Edward III (1327-77). The kinds of cloth woven ranged from best blue Beverley cloth which sold at 5s 10d (29p) a yard in 1319 to Kendal cloth costing 4½d (2p) a yard a century later. The wage of a carpenter in the mid-fourteenth century was 5d a day and a cow cost from 9s to 10s 6d. Increasing quantities of cloth were exported in preference to wool, as this brought more profit to the merchant and higher customs duties to the king. This led to the formation of the Merchant Adventurers Company in London in 1486, which controlled cloth exports to northern Europe. Cloth was made in every county but the bulk of the exports were drawn from three areas—good quality broadcloths from the West of England (Gloucestershire, Somerset, Wiltshire and Devon), worsteds from East Anglia (Norfolk, Suffolk and Essex) and coarse woollens from the West Riding of Yorkshire. The growth of the home industry in the fourteenth and fifteenth centuries meant that monasteries and landowners increasingly sold their wool to wool merchants, who sold the wool to the manufacturers in the markets and fairs held in medieval towns. Many new towns appeared as a result of the growth of the woollen industry. Halifax, for example, was unknown in the fourteenth century, had become a prominent cloth producing town by 1469 and was the principal cloth town in the West Riding in 1474. This was mainly because the parish of Halifax was one of the largest in the country, twelve miles long and several wide. There were many swift streams within the parish which provided ideal sites for fulling mills, and the infertile soils and lack of alternative employment encouraged most families to supplement their income with cloth production. Bradford, Wakefield, and Pontefract in Yorkshire, Frome in Somerset, Bradford-on-Avon in Wiltshire, Tiverton, Cullompton and Crediton in Devon were among many others that owed new prosperity to the increased demand for English cloth. Wool and cloth made up three-quarters of the value of exports in the fifteenth century. Edward III (1327–77) encouraged the industry by offering privileges to immigrants from Holland and Flanders who were skilled in finishing cloth. He stopped the import of foreign cloth and compelled everyone (except himself) to wear woollen cloth. The production of woollen cloth increased rapidly as a result, and the exports of cloth trebled between 1355 and 1395. The industry remained prosperous for a while, declined during the civil wars of the Roses and began to revive in the 1480s.

Changes in the industry in the sixteenth and seventeenth centuries were closely linked with changes in the supply of wool. The exports of raw wool dwindled almost to nothing by the 1580s as increasing quantities were made into cloth in Britain. The main wool producers were landowners by this time because the monasteries were closed down by Henry VIII in the 1530s and their land granted to private individuals. (Many villagers either rented land or had the right to graze sheep on common land.

They kept two or three sheep, perhaps up to twenty. It is impossible to calculate how much wool was produced like this but it was probably all used to clothe people in the village.) At Henry's death in 1547 40,000 families had some part of the monastery lands which had once totalled more than a quarter of England and Wales. Many of the new landowners decided that grazing sheep was the most profitable way of using their land. Sir Henry Fermor of East Barsham in Norfolk had twenty flocks, a total of 15,500 sheep. Some landowners deliberately turned arable land into sheep walks. Many people living in villages in Oxfordshire and neighbouring counties had their homes pulled down before their eyes and their fields filled with sheep, while they were left to find work and a house where they could.

This enforced closure of villages lessened during Elizabeth's reign (1558–1603) for the sale of cloth to Europe declined, especially from 1551 to 1575. This decline was mostly a natural slump in trade, made the more serious by the wars that affected most countries. The fall-off in world trade was sufficiently serious in 1557 for parliament to go to the aid of weavers in the traditional woollen towns by banning the production of cloth in rural areas unless it was for the use of the family. This was done by limiting rural families to one loom in the house; the fine for disobeying was a crushing 20s a week. The demand for cloth continued to grow in England to match a rising population. The export trade was further hindered when a London alderman called Cockayne persuaded James I to ban all exports of unfinished cloth from 1613 in the hope that it would encourage better dyeing and finishing in England. In fact the ban only served to encourage the expert finishers in Holland to produce their own cloth and, although the ban was lifted in 1617, cloth exports did not revive until after 1660. Increasingly, the yarn spinners obtained their wool a stone or two at a time from wool-broggers or chapmen who bought large quantities after the summer shearing and sold it by the pound all through the year.

The manufacture of worsted cloth increased rapidly in the seventeenth century. (Although made from wool the processes are very different from those used to make woollen cloth and are described below. The word "woollen" has to serve both meanings.) This increase was matched by a drastic reduction in the production of woollen cloths. The principal cause of this was a steady and irreversible change in the quality of English wool. The wool available in the Middle Ages had been short and springy, ideal for making woollen cloth. Most wool had become long and coarse by the mid-eighteenth century, and could no longer make the same high quality of cloth that had made English cloth so popular in Europe. The long wool could be used to make worsteds, and more of these were made in East Anglia and in Yorkshire. This was encouraged by refugees from France and Holland who were knowledgeable in this craft. Wool for the more expensive kinds of woollen cloth was imported from Spain and Ireland but both this and worsteds were for the wealthy alone to buy. Despite all the changes, more woollen cloth was made than worsted up to 1750, even though much of it was coarse and whiskery. It was cheap, though, and the best that most people in this country and the other European countries could afford.

WOOLLEN CLOTH PROCESSES

Weaving had reached a high standard by the seventh century; many dyes could be made and complex patterns woven. This was often all that noble ladies were allowed as recreation but it indicates higher standards in cloth production generally. There were even some attempts at large-scale production. An Anglo-Saxon weaving shed was excavated at Upton in Northamptonshire measuring thirty feet by eighteen. There had been two warp weighted looms, where the warp threads had been hung from a beam linking the two uprights. The threads were weighted with pottery rings, which were kept on racks against one wall. At least four women would have been needed to spin enough yarn to keep each loom going, as they used the slow drop spindle. With the other processes to be done as well, between ten and twenty people would have been kept in work. Many would have worked in their own homes, and the shed was home for the weavers.

The first step in preparing wool for spinning was to clean it and sort the fine wool from the coarse. The locks of wool were separated with hand cards. In Roman times these had been made of a number of teazles (like thistle heads) held in a wooden frame but these had given way to brass wire hooks by the twelfth century, which were in turn replaced by iron wire in the fifteenth century. Carding broke up the locks and formed an even sliver of wool. Slivers were joined together and wound on to a stick called a distaff, which could be tucked under one arm. The wool could now be spun, a process that blended twisting with drawing out to make a strong yarn. The drop spindle was no more than a straight stick with a pottery or stone weight on one end that could act as a flywheel. The spindle was spun between finger and thumb, and fibres were paid out to it from the sliver as evenly as possible. The weight of the spindle helped to draw them out. The yarn was wound on to the spindle when it reached the ground, fastened with a slip knot, and spinning began again. Such a tedious task was slow but could be done while walking around.

The warp threads were doubled on the loom since they had to give strength to the piece of cloth. The weft thread was woven in and out, and pushed as tight against the previous thread as could be. The piece was taken out of the loom when completed and washed in stale urine to dissolve the sheep's grease. It was then fulled—trampled under foot in a shallow pan of water and soapy fuller's earth, which felted the fibres together, making the cloth stronger and warmer. The cloth was stretched out on a tenter frame to dry to prevent shrinkage. Dyeing was done either before spinning ('dyed in the wool') or after tentering (piece dyed). The nap was raised with teazles, cropped with heavy shears, and the cloth was pressed ready for the customer.

Spinning was improved in the fourteenth century with the introduction of a spinning wheel known as the great wheel. This allowed better control over the wool when drawing it out and made a tighter twist. It was still a slow business and spinning seven pounds of wool was a week's work. The Saxony or Scots wheel appeared about 1480 and, when it was fitted with treadle drive early in the sixteenth century, made possible the most even kind of yarn yet, since both hands were free to draw out the fibres. The fact that new tools were available did not mean that the old methods were discarded at once; the distaff was still being used in Norfolk in 1800.

Two other major improvements spread into the industry in the Middle Ages. One was the frame loom which came into use about the end of the fourteenth century. The warp threads were paid out horizontally from a roller at the back of the loom to be wound on to a cloth roller at the front. Near the front of the loom, the warp threads passed through the eyes of healds. These were rectangular frames holding the many strings which kept the

Fig 9 *A cropper in his workshop. The pieces of cloth at the back have been hung up and raised*

eyes in place. The healds were arranged in the loom so that they could move vertically, pulled up or down by cords worked by treadles. The effect of this was that, with half the warp threads raised and the rest lowered, a gap was formed through which a shuttle could be passed in an instant—no more weaving the weft in and out. The weft thread unreeled from the shuttle as it was passed through the gap (the shed), was beaten up hard against the rest of the woven cloth and the healds were reversed so that the next weft thread could be put in. These improvements in the loom made weaving quicker, and the cloth produced was more uniform. The other improvement, in the twelfth century, was the use of heavy hammers for fulling the cloth. These had to be driven by water power and were often installed in corn mills. Their use led to the dispersal of the industry from the woollen centres of the Middle Ages in search of suitable streams. A machine that made less impact was the gig-mill, invented in the fifteenth century, to raise the nap on cloth. The cloth was drawn over a teazle-covered roller revolving in the opposite direction. Its use was banned by Edward VI (1547–53) because it aggravated unemployment, and it was still a target for demonstrators in the nineteenth century. Similar opposition discouraged the use of the stocking knitting frame invented by William Lee in 1589 and the ribbon loom developed in Danzig in 1604. Both came into wider use in the East Midlands by the eighteenth century, by which time they were used with linen, cotton and silk rather than wool.

The industry was so widespread that there were regional differences in its organisation. In the West Country, for example, the cloth merchants controlled output. They bought up the wool after shearing, their agents distributed it to spinners, delivered the yarn to weavers, and the cloth was put out on commission for both fulling and finishing. Farming was such a major occupation that this additional domestic industry was secondary. Farming in the West Riding of Yorkshire, by contrast, was difficult and unproductive. Cloth production was at least as important by the sixteenth century and the clothiers controlled production. They owned their looms and often their homes, bought the wool weekly from the broggers, had it spun by the family and others as necessary, wove it, took it to the mill for fulling and sold it un-

finished. The cloth merchants had it finished to their requirements. Between these two extremes there were many local
variations as to who controlled production and owned the tools
and wool. The one constant fact was that all the processes except
fulling and dyeing were done in people's homes, making them
cottage factories.

Early in the sixteenth century a handful of wealthy merchants
set up larger factories. John Winchcombe of Newbury is said to
have had 200 handlooms in one room and large numbers of
people worked at the other processes in proportion. John Stumpe
bought Malmesbury Abbey after the dissolution and installed
several hundred looms. The numbers are probably wildly exaggerated but indicate production methods very different from a
cottage-factory. The output of such places was an insignificant
part of the total.

The expansion of the industry in the first half of the sixteenth
century established the West Country and West Riding as the
principal areas producing cloth for export. Most areas continued
to produce their own cloths, however, though there was a growing internal trade between regions, in such goods as Welsh
flannel. Some of these areas exported small quantities, such as
the bright and cheap Lancashire woollens exported to France,
Spain and Portugal c 1560. The export trade declined in the
seventeenth century, as mentioned above, revived briefly in the
1650s, and declined again.

About fifty craftsmen arrived from Flanders in the 1660s and
brought new ways of dyeing cloth, and the use of Spanish wool
for the weft and English for the warp, which made a presentable
cloth. The industry was struggling to hold on to its traditional
dominance in the economy. Merchants persuaded parliament to
aid it with laws—compulsory burial in a woollen shroud was
ordered in 1667, imports of printed cotton were banned in 1700,
the use of cotton was prohibited in 1721. These were desperate
measures by men who had seen wealth in the country's dominant
industry and could not understand the changes in fashion and
production possibilities. The laws did little for the woollen industry which was replaced by cotton as the principal textile
industry about 1800. The production of woollen cloth for daily

use and for export continued to be important—the industry may not have expanded so fast but neither did it noticeably decline.

WORSTED PRODUCTION

Worsted cloth is also made from wool but the appearance of the cloth and therefore some of the processes are different. The cloth is smooth and every thread is visible. The raw wool was combed instead of carded. The combs were heated over charcoal fires and the wool was combed repeatedly to remove the short wool (noils) and leave the long fibres (tops) parallel with each other. These were taken from the combs and made into slivers. Spinning was done best by the Scots wheel and the fine yarn was woven on the same kind of loom as woollen cloth. No fulling was done, as worsted cloth is smooth to the touch. The cloth was finished by dyeing and pressing.

The wool used in the Middle Ages was from Lincolnshire sheep, which in part explains why the industry developed in East Anglia. (All English wool was suitable by the eighteenth century, allowing expansion of production.) The combers were the key men, since the quality of the combing determined the quality of the cloth. The master combers had complete control over production and therefore determined who had work and who went without.

Little worsted cloth was made until the end of the sixteenth century, for it was expensive. Religious refugees from Holland brought secrets of the 'new draperies', which were made with a combed warp and carded weft. This made a lighter cloth than woollens and, as knowledge of vegetable dyes such as madder, alder and woad increased, made possible the production of many patterns. There were many new cloths, with names like shalloons, sayes, bayes, serges, minikins, bombasines and many more. Combing skill was needed to make these and the immigrants settled among the worsted makers. Both the draperies and worsteds were produced in increasing quantities during the seventeenth century, and much was exported to the Mediterranean, Spain, Portugal and north Europe.

Yorkshire clothiers began to produce worsteds during the Commonwealth, and Halifax became the centre of the trade.

Production increased so fast in Yorkshire that it equalled that of East Anglia by 1750. Yorkshire was well placed after that time to take advantage of the new machinery developed for the cotton industry.

LINEN

The household officers of the Welsh courts in the seventh century were given three sets of clothes a year—the king gave the woollen cloth and the queen the linen. In the tenth century linen was preferred in England for underclothes and Saxon women were famed for their embroidery on linen. The best linen available in the eleventh century was imported from Flanders, and the quality of the home product declined and woollen cloth was preferred. The manufacture of fine linen began again in Wiltshire and Sussex in the thirteenth century—Henry III bought 1,000 ells (1,250 yards) in each county in 1253 to encourage the industry. Linen remained the only soft fabric available until cotton was imported in the seventeenth century. A heavier kind of linen was canvas, which was increasingly in demand as shipping developed.

Linen was made from the fibrous stem of flax. Flax production was encouraged by laws at intervals—one rood in every sixty tillable acres had to be sown with flax and hemp seed by an act of 1531. The flax was retted, hammered and drawn through iron combs to separate the fibres, a process called hackling. (The waste fibre—tow—was used to caulk ships.) Spinning and weaving used the same tools as the woollen industry. Linen could be dyed but first had to be bleached. Pieces were washed in alkali, soaked in sour milk and laid out on the ground to bleach, which took five to eight months. This was usually done by farmers and the first large-scale bleachfield, in Scotland, was not started until 1715.

Many Acts were passed in the seventeenth century to encourage the linen industry in England and Ireland. Imports of French linen were banned and in 1699 the Trustees for the Linen and Hempen Manufactures were set up in Dublin to encourage the industry by any means. A similar Board of Manufactures was appointed in Scotland in 1727 to encourage both linen and coarse wool production. It gave prizes for good examples of cloth and established spinning schools, particularly in the highlands. Each school was allowed £10, spent as follows:

mistress' salary	5.	0. 0
14 spinning wheels at 5s. 10d.	4.	1. 8
repairs (bands, pirns)		5. 0
coal and candle		13. 4

These schools met from October to April and did much to encourage linen production. However, the cotton industry was developing at this time, despite laws against it. Linen and cotton were very similar and the struggle for supremacy lasted for most of the eighteenth century.

COTTON

Cotton cloth was introduced to this country by the East India Company, which started in 1600. Known as calico, it was expensive but popular because of the bright colours it was dyed and cheerful patterns it was printed (neither of which could be done with wool). The ban on imported printed cotton in 1700 encouraged merchants to import it plain and have it dyed and printed in England. The imports of raw cotton began about this time. Cotton manufacture was discouraged for a time when the use of calico was prohibited in 1721 but an exception was made in 1736 for the mixed cloth fustian (cotton warp, linen or wool weft) and cotton manufacturing increased steadily regardless of the law.

Manufacturing was mostly carried on in Lancashire and adjoining parts of Cheshire and Yorkshire. There were several reasons for this. The ports of Chester and, later, Liverpool traded with many of the areas from which raw cotton was obtained—mainly the Middle East and America. This made it convenient to bring the cotton back to these ports. Although woollens had been woven in Lancashire, they were cheap goods and never very profitable. It did not take much to persuade the people who had carried on that business to switch instead to cotton, which promised to bring them better prices and wages. Nearly all the skills used in woollen cloth making were needed for cotton, so there was little hardship as a result of the change. Cotton was also imported through London, Bristol and Glasgow and cotton manufacturing started in all these areas also. Nowhere, though, had the incentives presented to the people of Lancashire to turn wholeheartedly to producing cotton goods. Even the local climate helped, Lancashire's damp air making it easier to prevent the fine yarn from breaking. Many skilled people were available as the local woollen industry was depressed. Cotton velvets, thicksets and other fabrics were made early in the century.

Production methods were similar to the woollen industry. The cotton was carded, spun and woven using the same tools, then bleached and dyed or printed. The bulk of the work was done as domestic industry with the merchants controlling output, and therefore controlling wages and availability of work. Control of the industry being in a few hands was to be important when expensive new machinery became available.

SILK

Silk was always a luxury fabric and its production was on a small scale. It was woven in Spitalfields, London, from imported Italian yarn in the seventeenth century, and the weavers were reinforced with many French refugees after Louis XIV had deprived French Protestants of their civil liberties by his revocation of The Edict of Nantes in 1685.

Silk manufacture was stimulated by John Lombe, who learnt by industrial espionage how silk was thrown in Italy and built a mill in Derbyshire to house his machines. The mill was built in 1718 on an island in the Derwent river, and was a wonder of the times. Three hundred people were employed there and silk mills were soon built in Macclesfield, Manchester and elsewhere. The thread mostly went to London for weaving or stocking knitting, and imports of French silk slowly declined.

PLACES TO VISIT

Despite the importance of the woollen industry, there is still no national museum for it, and therefore nowhere that the interested person may visit to see a comprehensive display of the development of the industry in Britain. The weaver's cottage at Kilbarchan, Renfrew, and the weaving workshop in the Colne

Page 69 (*above*) A fifteenth-century iron forge. The anvil is just a block on a wooden stand, and the visible tools are hammers and tongs. The method of working the bellows is clearly seen; (*below*) a tower mill on flat land facing the sea, so that the mill could be worked by the changing land and sea breezes. The fan tail can turn the cap by gears so that the sails face into the wind.

(*above*) Though many water wheels were placed on the outside wall of mills, many were enclosed and these were often very powerful. This wheel produced 60hp, sufficient to power the woollen mill it was in. Note the governor (left) for regulating the speed; (*below*) This 10hp beam engine represents the general-purpose engine that came into use early in the nineteenth century. It is made of heavy iron castings but is similar in appearance to eighteenth-century beam engines built of wood. The governor and parallel motion can be seen to mid-left and top right.

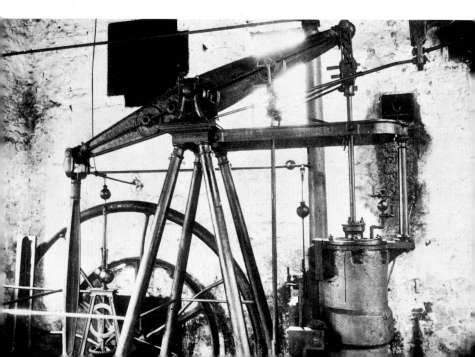

Valley Museum, Golcar, Huddersfield, give some idea of working conditions in a cottage factory, though of different periods. There are some interesting machines and more interesting models in the Science Museum, London. The collections of clothing in the Museum of Costume, Bath; Castle Howard Costume Gallery, Yorkshire, and the Gallery of English Costume, Manchester, all start with the seventeenth century. See also the museums listed at the end of this book and the end of chapter 15.

7 More Mines

The dyepans used in the woollen industry were made of iron and fired with coal in the sixteenth century. Brass wire was used for cards and iron wire later. There were many other uses for these and other metals and it will be simpler to separate them.

IRON

The principal iron mining areas in the Middle Ages were still the Weald and Forest of Dean, though smaller quantities were mined elsewhere. It was mined and smelted at Kirkby Overblows (ore-blowers) from the thirteenth century, for example, and the Forest of Knaresborough was consumed as charcoal in time. The ore was extracted by men using shovels and mattocks (broad-bladed pickaxes). Bloomeries (see p 29) continued to be used to smelt iron until 1700, despite their limitations. Only one bloom could be made at a time, and the foot-operated bellows used at most bloomeries had to be worked constantly to produce even that. The Bishop of Durham installed water-driven bellows in 1408 but even so, it does not seem that these enabled the melting-point of iron to be reached. Smelters continued to use bloomeries even after the bigger blast furnaces had been proved successful. The reason was not obstinacy. Bloomeries were a cheaper way of making wrought iron, which was the kind of iron most in demand for tools, hinges, bars, nails and most other things. After the bloom was taken from the furnace it was hammered repeatedly to remove the slag it still contained. The result was wrought iron, which could later be hammered and filed to shape and would withstand rough treatment.

The uses of iron were infinite. Sheffield was renowned for

arrow heads and knives in 1297, and the Gloucester fair was famed in the fourteenth century for its agricultural tools. Every village blacksmith made horse shoes and the daily requirements of the community. The king and monasteries provided most of the money needed to build furnaces and forges. In 1255–6, for example, the king drew £58 5s 1d (£58.25½) from his forges and mines in the Forest of Dean, and Tintern Abbey had mines and a forge in the forest and another forge at the abbey.

Fig 10 *Blacksmiths shaping scythe and sickle blades*

Many improvements came in the sixteenth century when skilled German workers were encouraged to settle in Britain. They knew how to make the best use of large blast furnaces. The first was set up in Britain in 1490 but there were only six by 1540; there were 120 in 1600, half of them in the Weald and Surrey. A survey was made in 1635 of all the forges and furnaces in the Forest of Dean, which gives the size and value of these furnaces:

Cannop Furnace—Now blowinge, and likely to contynue aboute 3 weeks. The most part new built, and the rest repaired by the Farmers [those renting the furnaces] about 4 years since. Stone walls, about 6olb [ie £60], consistinge of the stone body thereof 22 foote square . . . A Wheele, 22 foote diameter, 7 iron Whops [hoops], one the Waste [waist], made about 3 years since. With shafte and all things belonging about 2olb, in good repaire . . .

The wheel drove a pair of large bellows, each eighteen feet by four. The surveyor went on to list all the buildings, workers' houses and tools, which gives a clear impression of the layout of such an iron works.

The draught from these big bellows made the furnace hot enough to melt the iron. This meant that the furnace could be run continuously for several weeks, filling it alternately with iron ore and fuel. The molten iron was tapped from the bottom, run into shallow pits in the ground and allowed to solidify into pigs. These could be taken to a finery where they could be forged (repeatedly heated and hammered) into wrought iron. This was a roundabout way of making wrought iron compared with a bloomery, but the bigger blast furnace could make a greater quantity of iron at one time. Pig iron could also be remelted and used to make castings, with the aid of the same kind of patterns and moulds that the bronze workers had used in Roman times. It was possible for the iron to be cast straight from the furnace if the mould could be brought near enough. Cast iron is brittle (because it contains about 4 per cent carbon) and cannot be hammered into shape or used to make anything that will need to be hammered. It was used to make firebacks, cooking pots, cannon—anything where the thickness of the metal was either an advantage or did not matter.

74

Most iron produced in Britain was forged into bar-iron, a third of which was passed through slitting mills to make nails. England produced 20,000 tons of iron in 1700. A further 17,300 tons (all of it bar-iron except 400 tons) were imported from Sweden to supply the country's needs. Home production could not increase until more reliable sources of power and an alternative to charcoal could be found. Timber was in great demand for house building, shipbuilding and everything else, and the iron industry was prevented from taking all the wood it wanted made into charcoal by the charcoal-burners.

The fuel problem was to a large extent overcome by Abraham Darby, as described in the following letter by his daughter-in-law in 1783:

> It was my husband's Father that attempted to mould and cast Iron pots, etc, in sand instead of Loam in which he succeeded at an Air Furnace in Bristol. About the year 1709 he came into Shropshire to Coalbrookdale. He here cast Iron Goods in sand out of the Blast Furnace that blow'd with wood charcoal. Sometime after he suggested the thought that it might be practable to smelt the Iron from the ore in the blast Furnace with Pit Coal. He first try'd with raw coal as it came out of the Mines, but it did not answer. He, not discouraged, had the coal coak'd into Cynder [coke], as is done for drying Malt, and it then succeeded to his satisfaction.

The use of coke for smelting was a major breakthrough; although the resulting iron could only be used for casting, this was the kind that had been most expensive. Darby's son, Abraham Darby II, added limestone to the smelting process which absorbed some of the impurities and made it possible to forge the iron. The result was a considerable increase in iron production and use, as will be seen in chapter 14.

NON-FERROUS METALS

The mining of lead, copper and tin was carried on in scattered areas and on a small scale in the Middle Ages. The Benedictine Repton Abbey mined lead at Wirksworth, Derbyshire, in the ninth century, and the Domesday Book (1086) records lead mining there and in the manors of Bakewell, Ashford and Hope. Lead mining continued in the Middle Ages—the customs and privileges of the Derbyshire miners were written down in 1288 as a guide to employment. Similarly, *The Laws and Customs of the Mine* regulated the Flintshire lead mines in 1352. Mining continued in the Mendips—there are references from 1189—but little solid fact has survived. Lead was widely used in building and to make pewter, and its silver was the basis of the English currency. Tin mining in Cornwall supplied the other metal for pewter but mining was minimal. In Carmarthenshire, monks at Talley Abbey ran a lead and silver mine and may also have operated the Dolau Cothi gold mine.

The sixteenth century saw changes in all these metals. Lead mines in central Wales were developed in mid-century, where a ton of lead contained sixty ounces of silver. (A mint was set up in Aberystwyth in the 1640s.) The Mendip mines were divided into four groups with accounting centres at Charterhouse, Chewton Mendip, East Harptree and Priddy. Two kinds of smelting hearth were used. One was a turn-hearth mounted on a wooden platform so that it could be turned into the wind. The other was similar to an iron furnace, with foot-operated bellows. German miners were encouraged to come to Britain by Elizabeth and later monarchs, bringing more efficient working methods. Gunpowder was used in German mines in 1670, and its use quickly spread to this country. The Dutchman Sir Cornelius Vermuyden was employed in the 1630s to dig the Cromford Sough to underdrain some Derbyshire mines. The demand for lead continued to increase into the eighteenth century and production increased in all the mining areas.

Tin mining produced an average of 450 tons a year from 1199 to the end of the fifteenth century, mostly in Devon and Cornwall. A slight increase in the sixteenth century became a substantial increase after 1675—an average of 1,400 tons were produced 1675–1750. The methods were noted by Celia Fiennes in 1698:

Halfe a mile from [St. Austel] they blow their tin which I went to see: they take the ore and pound it in a stamping mill which resembles the paper mills, and when it's fine as the finest sand . . . this they fling into a furnace and with it coale to make the fire, so it burns together and makes a violent heate and fierce flame, the mettle by the fire being separated from the coale and its own drosse, being heavy, falls down to a trench made to receive it, at the furnace hole below; this liquid mettle I saw them shovel up with an iron shovel and soe pour it into moulds in which it cooles and soe they take it thence in sort of wedges or piggs I think they call them; it's a fine mettle thus in its first melting looks like silver, I had a piece poured out and made cold for to take with me . . .

I went a mile farther on the hills and soe where they were digging in the Tinn mines, there was at least 20 mines all in sight which employs a great many people at work, almost night and day, but constantly all day and every day includeing the Lords day which they are forced to, to prevent their mines being overflowed with water; more than 1000 men are taken up about them, few mines but had then almost 20 men and boys attending it, either down in the mines digging and carrying the ore to the little bucket which conveys it up or else others are draineing the water and looking to the engines that are draineing it, and those above are attending the drawing up the ore in a sort of windless as is to a well.

The 'engines' draining the mines were waterwheels driving pumps. Thomas Savery's steam engine had only just been invented, and was little used (see below, p 86).

The copper industry was developed largely by one man, who laid the foundations for later prosperity. He was Daniel Hochstetter from Augsburg, who was given exclusive rights in 1564 to search for copper, gold and silver in the Lake District. Two partnership companies were formed in 1568 as a result. The Company of Mines Royal had the monopoly of copper mining in several counties and started in Keswick, Westmorland. Its richest mines were at Borrowdale and Newlands, with the smelting concentrated at Keswick. The output of the six mines in 1570 was 928cwt valued at £2,784 14s 5½d (£2,784.72). Hochstetter had wanted to export the ingots to Germany but as this was illegal the company made kettles and pans and distributed the remainder to Newcastle, Bristol and elsewhere. The company was always in difficulties and ran at a loss in 1600.

The Company of Mineral and Battery Works began in the valley above Tintern Abbey with a monopoly of brass and wire production. Brass and iron were battered through iron dies before being drawn out to make wire. Again the company was not immediately successful and many years of practice were needed to produce the right quality, aided by a law in 1672 forbidding the imports of wire. The use of copper for coinage began in 1578, when Bristol was allowed to mint its own farthings because of the shortage of low value coins—the smallest official coin was the silver penny. As with the woollen industry, the expansion of industrial activity came in the mid-sixteenth century and was based on adapting existing machines to use water power.

COAL

Coal was shipped from the Tyne from the end of the twelfth century. It was mined around Tynemouth, Gateshead and Whickham. The coal was often ballast in French and Flemish grain ships, as Newcastle's other exports were cloth, grindstones and fish. Coal was profitable as a cargo by the mid-thirteenth century but trade seldom exceeded 15,000 tons before 1500. In Scotland coal was mined in East Lothian and shipped to Edinburgh, Perth, Dundee and even Aberdeen and the islands. Coal was mined in other parts of England and Wales wherever it outcropped on or near the surface and where it could be used. Bellpit mining was almost always the method used, with some adit mining in the Tyne field.

Shipments of coal from Newcastle to London increased in the sixteenth century and coal was there known as sea-coal. It was used increasingly to heat vats for brewing, dyeing, soap and sugar boiling, as well as domestic fires. Elizabeth tried to limit coal burning because of the pollution and fire hazard but the shortage of timber left no alternative. Trade in sea-coal varied widely but averaged 500,000 tons a year by 1700. Coal was being mined in all the major areas except Kent by that time and production in the country reached an estimated $2\frac{1}{2}$ million tons. The methods used had not changed much except that some shafts were being dug. These were rare because of drainage problems and no real expansion took place in the industry until later in the eighteenth century.

TOOLS

Most tools were made of metal, or contained some. The farm

tools used from ancient times, for example, included the plough, which had a wooden frame reinforced with an iron share and, sometimes, coulter. Iron-shod spades, iron heads for picks and forks, and iron blades for sickles were common in Roman times and in the Middle Ages. The scythe came in the twelfth century. These formed the basic agricultural tools and had hardly changed by the eighteenth century. The spade became an all-iron blade and billhooks were developed for hedges. Jethro Tull's seed drill and hoe led to a wider use of metal in more specialised tools but mostly later in the century.

Iron was the main metal in the blacksmith's workshop, for anvil, tongs, hammers and wire-drawing dies. Engraved punches were used by coiners. Carpenters in the first century used adzes, axes and knives for rough shaping, and had the plane, bow-drill and brace, as well as handsaws, rasps and files. In addition to massive tables and chests, stick furniture was common from the Middle Ages. Wood for this kind of furniture was turned on a pole lathe, which was used from the seventh to the seventeenth century. A piece of cord was wound round the piece of wood to be turned, and tied to a foot pedal below and to the end of a springy pole above. The turner cut the wood as he pressed down on the pedal; the pole pulled the cord up for him to repeat the process. The treadle lathe began to be used in the sixteenth century. Apart from nails, braces and drills, all tools were made by the blacksmith and were jealously guarded by a joiner as valuable private property.

PLACES TO VISIT

The museum in Battle, Sussex, has a collection of local ores, etc, and there is a number of machines and their products in the collection in Bishop Hooper's Lodging, Gloucester. The use of metals for weapons and armour are illustrated in the Castle Museum, Pontefract, and Ludlow Museum, Shropshire, and many stately homes open to the public. Abraham Darby's furnaces are preserved as part of the Ironbridge Gorge Museum, Telford. The Museum of English Rural Life, Reading, has a national collection of agricultural tools and household objects, and an eighteenth-century woodworker's shop has been reconstructed in the Geffrye Museum, London.

8 Commercial Chemicals

Textiles and metals were the largest industries in this period, employing the greatest numbers and contributing most to the economy. There were other industries whose level of production could never approach these but whose products were necessary. Some of these smaller industries took root at the end of the fifteenth century, others had a longer history.

PAPER AND PRINTING
The small quantities of paper used in the Dark Ages for royal and church accounts and records were imported from China via Arab merchants. Imports came from Italy in the twelfth century and were supplemented by a poorer quality paper from Germany in the fourteenth. Paper manufacture caught on late in Britain, perhaps in the sixteenth century. One of the oldest known mills was Warnford Mill, built in 1618 in Hampshire, which made brown paper to be sold by Southampton stationers. The industry was encouraged by the development of printing in the sixteenth century and the popularity of wallpaper after 1650.

The ingredients of paper were cotton, linen, straw and wood, which were pounded by water-powered stamps (heavy timbers arranged vertically, raised by cogs and allowed to fall on the materials). The fibres were mixed with water, transferred to a vat and stirred constantly to prevent settling. The maker dipped in a rectangular frame which held a bottom of tightly stretched wire mesh. The fibres felted together as the water drained through and the sheet was peeled off and laid between pieces of felt. These were piled up to a gross and pressed for twenty-four hours to squeeze out the water. The sheets were hung to dry in a draughty loft. Rubbing with a stone, or sizing with tanner's waste made a smoother surface. Wooden rollers were used to finish the surface from 1700.

Printing followed a similar pattern. All books were copied by hand (mostly in the monasteries) until the press was introduced to Europe about 1450. It developed fast, so that more books were produced in 1450–1500 than in the previous thousand years. The first press in England was set up by William Caxton in 1476, to be followed by many others. British printers gained some advantages in starting up later than much of Europe, in that the significant developments had been made and they could start with methods that were to last into the nineteenth century. The press, for example, had already had the tympan added to place the paper exactly over the type (Fig 11). Subsequent changes were little more than fitting rails to withdraw the bed. Ink made of boiled linseed oil and lamp black or powdered charcoal was available, and the use of movable type instead of each word being carved separately was common. Lead alloy was used to make the letters in the sixteenth century and the number of joined letters was steadily reduced (fi and ffi are examples of joined letters still in use). Type was set by hand, locked in an iron frame (a chase) and put in the press. No other significant changes were made in printing methods before 1750.

Fig 11   *A handpress. The hinged flap is the tympan*

The Romans had preferred to import good quality glassware from the Rhineland which, with Normandy, continued to be the centre for most of England's needs in the Middle Ages. This may well have continued unbroken from the fifth century for the glass made by the Jutes in Kent was poor stuff. Workers from Normandy built glass kilns in the forests of Surrey and the Weald in 1226 and the industry developed from there. Green glass both for windows and vessels was made at Chiddingfold in the thirteenth and fourteenth centuries, and in Staffordshire at Bromley Hurst (1289–1420) and Wolseley (1418–77). As in many trades, glass making was combined with farming. Timber was needed both as fuel and as potash, for glass was melted from sand, potash and lime. Bottles and bowls were made, often tinted green or brown by impurities. Churches mostly had glazed windows by the thirteenth century though it was found in only the largest houses before 1450. Round sheets were made by spinning molten glass on an iron rod, which left the characteristic blob (the crown) in the centre. Glass could be stained by the addition of chemicals—copper produced green and red glass, gold chloride the finest red, iron gave brown and yellow, and these could be combined. The art of making stained-glass windows reached its peak in the Middle Ages, as a visit to some older churches can show.

The most sought after glass came from Venice, where the secrets of crystal glass were known. A number of Venetians came to Britain in the sixteenth century, and also workers from France and Flanders, attracted by a growing market for glassware. Jean Carre of Antwerp received a London licence to make window and crystal glass in 1567, which passed in 1572 to a Venetian, Jacob Verselini. Glass furnaces were built in many parts of England and the glass made became both better in quality and cheaper. The improved quality meant there was less waste, and improvements in furnace design reduced fuel costs. Wood was banned to the industry in 1615 and furnaces had to be adapted to burn coal. In 1675 George Ravenscroft began to produce lead crystal glass which became very popular, as did engraved bowls and drinking glasses. The French way of casting plate glass was not copied in Britain until 1773, however.

There was nothing like a chemical industry in the twentieth century sense, though there were a number of producers of some chemicals. Salt, for example, was needed in large quantities in the Middle Ages to preserve fish and meat. Whitby Abbey had its own salt pans, where sea water was boiled on coal fires in lead pans until crystals formed. The need for salt continued long after the monasteries were closed, and pans were erected on the Tyne estuary, the Ayrshire coast (Saltcoats), at Lymington in Hampshire and elsewhere. The sun was used for evaporation for four months in the year at Lymington, which helped to offset the high cost of Newcastle coal. At the peak of its prosperity in about 1750, 50,000 tons were produced a year. Natural brine springs were evaporated in Worcestershire and Cheshire in the sixteenth century, and rock salt was found in Cheshire in 1690.

Most other chemicals were produced for the textile industry. Copperas, for example, was derived from iron pyrites and used to produce black dyes—the only dye permitted for flat caps by a law of 1565. A by-product of making copperas was sulphuric acid, which led to an expansion of copperas production in the mid-eighteenth century. Another example was the expansion of soap-boiling to serve the needs of cloth-fulling. The best soap was made from Mediterranean olive oil but whale oil was increasingly used from the end of the seventeenth century. In 1615 a bright scarlet dye was found by adding a salt made by dissolving pewter in nitric acid to red cochineal. Other examples can be found of localised chemical producers, almost always arising out of the needs of the woollen industry.

PLACES TO VISIT

Examples of glass can be seen at the Ryedale Folk Museum, Hutton-le-Hole, Yorkshire. Saxon pottery is kept at the Ancient House Museum, Thetford, Norfolk, and later pottery in Rye Museum, Sussex, and Nottingham City Museum. The work of builders can be seen in houses restored at the Weald and Downland Open Air Museum, Chichester, and the Welsh Folk Museum, St Fagan's, Cardiff. Many ancient houses still stand where they were built, and some of the older churches have their stained-glass windows.

9 Wind and Water

Some kind of power is needed to make anything. It may be no more than the muscles of a child grinding flour but it is still power. In Roman times and for long afterwards the efforts of men and animals were the only available sources of power for most tasks, though alternative sources could have been used. Most jobs were done by muscle power, which had its limitations. Animals, especially oxen, were the stronger and were used to draw ploughs and reaping machines in Roman times, and for transport. Oxen, mules and, rarely, horses were harnessed to gins, which were horizontally mounted windlasses winding a rope over the heads of the animals. Gins were used to lift ore from mines and in drainage. More directly, they were harnessed to grindstones to grind flour and to edge-running stones to crush apples for cider and logwoods for cloth dyes. Animals could continue with such heavy and repetitive work for long hours but needed stops for food and rest.

Human muscles were far less powerful but more adaptable. The range of chisels handled by a stonemason or woodcarver and their achievements in medieval cathedrals illustrates the point. Many parts of manufacturing processes requiring less skill also had to be done by people, either because animals could not be used or could not be afforded. Many women ground their own corn in hand querns until the eleventh century, for example, and the bellows of iron furnaces were normally worked by foot. All cloth was fulled by feet until the twelfth century, and all other woollen processes were done by hand.

There were obvious drawbacks to seeking power from men and animals. Their strength was limited both in scale and duration, and any continuous process needing power was out of the question. Men as well as animals were frequently worked until they dropped, and lives were grossly shortened in consequence, but there was a limit to the amount of power that could be extracted from such sources. Neither source provided a constant supply of power, making it pointless to devise any machine that needed to be run at a constant speed.

Early water wheels improved on some of these gaps. They saved some of the killing drudgery and provided a source of power that could be developed far beyond that of oxen. There were water wheels in Britain in Roman times and it seems that they introduced them to Britain. The wheels were undershot, that is they were fitted with paddles which dipped into the stream (Fig 12). The movement of water turned the wheel. Such

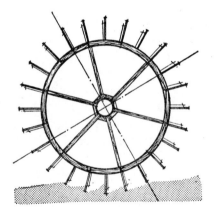

UNDERSHOT WATERWHEEL

Fig 12

wheels are known to have been used for corn grinding in Lincoln, along Hadrian's Wall and at Woolaston Pill in Gloucestershire. The Romans used overshot wheels in some parts of the Empire but there is no evidence of any in Britain. An overshot wheel has buckets around the rim and the water is brought to the top of the wheel by a wooden trough, variously called flume,

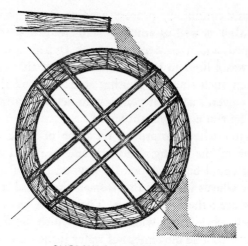

OVERSHOT WATERWHEEL

Fig 13

launder or goit (Fig 13). The wheel is turned both by the movement of the water and by its weight.

In the Scottish highlands and in Ireland a horizontal wheel was used (Fig 14). This was mounted beneath the mill and was driven by a jet of water being taken from the stream by a trough. The axle passed up through the floor of the mill to drive a single

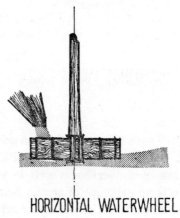

HORIZONTAL WATERWHEEL

Fig 14

Page 87 (*above*) An example of a specialised steam engine, of the kind developed over many years for the textile mills. It was built in 1901 and produced 1,600hp. The fly-wheel was 24ft, and 42 ropes drove the spinning mules on several floors; (*below*) a steam turbine installed in 1917 to produce electricity. It produces all the power needed to drive machinery in two woollen mills.

Page 88 (above) Coal wagons moving by gravity from South Hetton to Seaham. The loaded train pulled the empty wagons back; (below) a collier on his way to work. A beam engine is draining the mine. The locomotive is one of several built by Mathew Murray for John Blenkinsop in 1812, to take coal from Middleton to Leeds. The centre driving wheel had cogs, engaging with others on the outside of the rails.

pair of grindstones. Such mills were in use in Ireland in the seventh century and were common in all the Viking colonies. The last surviving one is in the Orkneys. Although built and maintained by someone, the mills were for the common use of all and there were no tolls to be paid. Horizontal wheels could be adapted for other industrial uses though not as easily as the overshot wheels.

The number of water powered corn mills increased in the Dark Ages. There were several in Winchester in 983, while the Domesday Book (1086) recorded 5,624 mills, most of which will have been water powered. It is likely that the great majority were corn mills but the rent of two Somerset mills was paid in blooms of iron, suggesting water-driven bellows. Some of the mills were undoubtedly of the traditional kind, with a wheel mounted vertically on the outside of a small building. Others went further by having streams dammed to make a mill pond, to guarantee sufficient power from a small stream. Some mills only operated in the winter months when streams were full. In sheltered coastal areas mills were operated by the tides, while water wheels mounted between two pontoons were anchored in the Thames.

Increasing numbers of water mills were built or enlarged in the Middle Ages. Each belonged to the lord of the manor, and the villagers had to have their corn ground there and pay a toll to the miller (commonly a sixteenth by weight). The lord of the manor had to keep the mill in repair, which could be expensive. Flooding could wreck a water wheel and also do considerable damage to machinery in the mill. The power was normally taken off by a lantern gear wheel meshing on the teeth of a pit gear on the same shaft as the wheel. These were made of wood and could be warped by water.

Although most mills were for grinding corn other uses were found for water power during the Middle Ages. Cloth fulling was possible by water driven stocks by the end of the twelfth century which were used increasingly as the woollen industry expanded. The stocks were a pair of mallets on stout arms, together weighing many hundredweight. They were lifted alternately by cogs on a tappet wheel, which was fixed on the water wheel axle. The use of water power for fulling was instrumental in taking the woollen industry away from the traditional manufacturing towns because of the pressure on available power supplies. Fulling was often accommodated in corn mills where spare room and power was available.

Tappet wheels were also used to raise tilt hammers in iron works, at least from the sixteenth century. These were worked at about 150 strokes a minute to shape reaping hooks and other edge tools, which were often a sandwich of hard steel between softer iron, making it possible to keep a sharp edge. They were sharpened by the dangerous practice of a man lying on a board suspended over a water powered grindstone. Bellows for blast furnaces had been water driven from the fifteenth century and fans, slitting and cutting mills where iron was flattened into sheets and cut into bars for making nails were developed in the seventeenth. Cable haulage of boats and wagons was in use by the eighteenth century and also water-powered pumps for mine drainage. The breast-shot wheel, developed in the sixteenth century, was increasingly used by this time. The weight of the water against paddles or in the buckets on the wheel still provided much of the power but the force of the water was also harnessed by making it turn the wheel to find a lower level. This was done by building walls close up to the wheel so that the water could not run to waste. This was the most efficient method of the three types of vertical wheel.

The last natural source of power to be harnessed was wind. This was used in most parts of Britain at some time or other despite its variable strength and direction. The first known windmill was in existence in 1185 at Weedley in Yorkshire. It was a post mill, a kind that continued to be built for centuries. The body of the mill, the buck, was mounted on a single oak post in such a way that it could turn in any direction. The post was fastened to two beams at right angles and so raised off the ground to avoid rotting. The arms nearly touched the ground, and the canvas sail had to be set on each one separately. The miller had to turn the buck by a long tail pole so that the sails faced into the wind. Power for grinding was taken off the shaft by gears. The only alterations made when post mills were built in the eighteenth century were that the base of the post was enclosed in a round-house of brick or stone and that sails were replaced by centrally adjustable canvas shutters.

Long before this, early in the fifteenth century, the first tower mill had been built at Burton Dasset in Warwickshire. Tower mills were built of brick or stone and were at first no higher than post mills because canvas still had to be set on the sails from outside. Gradually they became taller, as the builders tried to find a flow of wind that was not made turbulent by other buildings, and a gallery was built from which the miller could set the sails. Mills were built taller still in the eighteenth century to house more sets of grindstones. John Smeaton's device for opening and closing shutters on the sails from inside the mill took much of the danger from the miller's work; but his working time continued to be dictated by the moods of the weather. Similar mills were built of wood, and were called smock mills. In both, the sails and shaft were carried in the cap, which was free to turn in response to the wind. The construction of mills, involving the balancing of heavy weights and use of gears, made millwrights the engineers of the time.

Most windmills were built exclusively for grinding flour. Some were used in the eighteenth century for snuff grinding, and windmills were also vital for draining the Fens.

Drainage was the spur to the development of the first artificial form of power—steam. The immediate cause of the first steam engine was the need to drain mines in Devon and Cornwall, though a number of attempts to make steam engines had been made in England and France in the seventeenth century. (The Greeks had used a steam jet engine to open temple doors but the knowledge had been lost.)

Thomas Savery is credited with the discovery of the principle of the steam engine in about 1698. The first workable steam engine was built by Thomas Newcomen, a Dartmouth blacksmith in about 1709. Strictly speaking it was an atmospheric engine, for the working stroke was made by atmospheric pressure. Steam was used to raise the piston in the vertical cylinder, cold water sprayed into the cylinder condensed the steam, forming a vacuum, and atmospheric pressure forced the piston down again (Fig 15). The cylinder was open at the top. This up and down motion was excellent for pumping, and engines were set up in Cornish tin mines and Tyneside coal mines. The engine could not be used for anything else except by the laborious process of pumping water into a millpond with which to drive a water wheel. The engine was slow and heavy on coal but was the beginnings of a source of power that would transform industry and the lives of many people.

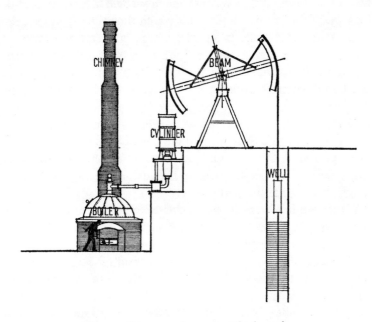

Fig 15 *Diagram of an atmospheric engine*

PLACES TO VISIT

Parts of a sixteenth-century water wheel are on show at the Abbeydale Industrial Hamlet, Sheffield, and the buildings of Preston Mill, East Linton, East Lothian, date from the same time though its machinery is more recent. Sarehole Mill, Birmingham, is an eighteenth-century corn mill. See also the museums listed at the end of the book.

10   Delivering the Goods

It is natural for us to think of roads first in any mention of transport as they are now the basis of the country's transport arrangements. They have not always been so, and the condition of the roads has been a constant cause of complaint.

The roads quickly decayed after the Romans left Britain in 410. The system had been planned to control a unified country and was irrelevant to the many independent tribes that lived in Britain. The Celtic peoples preferred hill top villages to the low-lying Roman towns and so were remote from most roads. They were better served by the Bronze Age ridgeways. The Roman system was largely ignored, apart from short lengths that came in useful here and there. Tree roots, frost, flooded streams, weeds and weathering soon reduced many of the roads to impassable tracks, and others were swallowed up in marshland.

In their place a network of rough tracks developed over a period of a thousand years. The slow increase in the population and in the amount of goods being moved necessitated the establishment of lines of communication between the cities and market towns, which was encouraged by the growing unification of England. Developments were slower in Wales, Ireland and Scotland.

These roads were not constructed, but were well-trodden routes that had become permanent tracks. A handful of them, linking London with the main cities of the Midlands, North and West, were regarded as king's highways. People had the right to travel on these in safety, under the king's protection. This was a necessary safeguard at a time when someone from the next village was regarded with suspicion as a foreigner. Little was done about the surface of the king's highways—travellers were guaranteed the right to go along that route, not any hope of travelling in comfort. If the road was impassable, travellers were allowed to take to the fields beside the road instead. The protection offered was not much better. Attempts were made to clear all bushes from the road verges, depriving highwaymen of hiding places. For the most part, though, 'protection' amounted to the punishments that would be meted out to anyone attacking a traveller—which was not much consolation to the victim. Even this amount of protection was not available on the great majority of roads and travellers used them at risk of ambush, broken axles and endless delay from obstructions.

Sporadic attempts were made to improve matters. Monasteries frequently built bridges and maintained roads in their immediate area, and the Church generally acted as agents for people bequeathing money for road improvements. Merchants increasingly took an interest in bridge building from the fourteenth century, and many towns improved the roads leading into them.

The roads were little used for most of the Middle Ages. The majority of people rarely left the parish in which they were born —there was too much work to do and no long holidays. Royal and Church officials, packmen visiting the fairs, and a steadily growing number of goods carriers made up most of the traffic. People travelled on foot or horseback, rarely in a carriage. Goods were carried mostly in panniers on pack animals, each pannier holding about a hundredweight, or were put across the animals' backs. Carts were rarely used. The cost of carriage remained constant from 1260 to 1540 at a penny per mile for a ton of grain and double for heavy loads like lead and tiles. This was very expensive—a farm labourer's wage in the thirteenth century averaged 2d a day. The long time taken over a journey, due to ruts, holes and obstruction on the road, added to the cost, making manufactured goods expensive.

The expansion of trade and industry in the sixteenth century required that something be done to improve the roads. No one took over the monks' interest when the monasteries were closed, and road surfaces were cut to pieces by increasing traffic. The Highways Act of 1555 tried to remedy matters by making each

94

parish responsible for the roads within it. A surveyor of the highways was elected to be responsible for all matters relating to roads and traffic, which included supervising all the able-bodied men of the parish who were obliged to work on the roads for a week each year. The scheme looked impressive but many parishes were content to keep the village main street passable and ignore the rest. They had neither funds nor technical skill to make sound roads out of cart tracks, and saw no reason to do so when they had no use for the roads themselves. Yet long distance traffic was increasing, and did so steadily in the seventeenth century. A flying coach service from London to Oxford began in 1669, travelling at just over four miles an hour. Most goods were still moved by pack animals, such as the strings that left Exeter every Saturday carrying cloth which arrived in London the following Friday. (The Roman road constructed 1,400 years before was used as far as Honiton, and was the easiest part of the journey.) Various attempts were made in the century to limit the weight of wagons to prevent damage to road surfaces but the growing volume of traffic made such limits ineffective. Localised improvements were made to the roads but the future lay with the turnpike trusts.

These were groups of local merchants and others who, backed by parliamentary approval, set about bringing the roads to a reasonable standard. They were allowed to erect gates across the road and collect tolls from passing traffic to pay for their work. The first trust was formed in 1706 and about 700 were active by 1760. These first trusts were mainly concerned to put a surface on the existing road and maintain it—few attempts at improving the route taken were made. Thus the roads were still only suited to pack animals and light vehicles, which could now travel rather more speedily. The costs of tolls were covered by the saving in time. There were not enough trusts to form a network of maintained roads by 1750 and the roads were still what they had been since Roman times, secondary to water transport in all parts outside the London area.

Though it is more natural for us to think of roads as the core of transport, their place was taken by water throughout the thirteen centuries of this section. Britain is well served by rivers that could take thirty to forty ton boats far inland. The sea has always been a useful if dangerous form of transport, and is still the basis of movement in some areas. Water transport was less subject to delays, which therefore reduced costs—cloth taken by road from Leeds to York in the seventeenth century cost four times as much per mile as it did when shipped from York to Hull on the river Ouse. Even water transport was expensive though—Newcastle coal which sold at the pithead for 5s (25p) a chaldron cost £2 5s —£2 10s when it reached Oxford via the North Sea and Thames. All the major towns of the Middle Ages were on rivers or near the sea, which made it possible for them to develop commercially. People were far more at home on water than they were on land— the hazards of water travel were less severe than those on land.

The coracle was probably the only kind of boat widely used after Roman times. It was made of thin laths interlaced and covered with hides. It was excellent for carrying one or two people, and small quantities of goods. Similar construction was used to make the much larger Irish currachs which, however frail in appearance, can still ride over Atlantic waves. The Vikings and other invaders arrived in the famous wooden longships, and Alfred had similar ships built to fight the Danes when he was king of Wessex. The longship had a strong keel into which the ribs of the ship were jointed. Planks were fastened to these with trenails (wooden pegs) starting from the keel, and each plank overlapped the one beneath it. Ships made by this method were described as clinker built, and were very strong. They were built all sizes, with the ruling proportion of the length being five times the width. There was one mast carrying a square sail, with rowers on each side when the wind was insufficient. The ship was steered with a long oar trailing over the right stern (the steerboard side, now starboard side). Alfred built ships to fight the Vikings but the open boats were as suitable for trade around the coasts and far inland, and Viking voyages in later centuries to Russia, the Mediterranean and America are well known.

The round ship was developed in the eleventh century, and was enlarged to the cog in the thirteenth. The proportions were twice as long as wide, making a ship that wallowed in the water and was hard to steer. Fitted at first with a single square sail, such boats were slow, awkward and dependent on a following wind. They were useful for carrying bulky cargoes such as wool, where speed was not vital. A triangular lateen sail made it possible to sail closer to the wind, and steering was improved with a rudder on the stern post. The cog was expanded into the carrack by the sixteenth century, which was about three times as long as it was wide. The carrack was carvel built, with high castles at bows and stern, and many more square and lateen sails. The planks making the hull of carvel-built ships fitted smoothly against one another instead of overlapping. Any gap between them were caulked with tar and pitch. The *Great Harry*, built at the command of Henry VIII, was 1,500 tons, had a crew of 900 and carried 195 'pop-guns' to fire at enemy boarders. This was exceptional but indicates the capabilities of shipbuilders who must have gained their experience constructing smaller boats for fishing and trade.

Shipyards were usually on river banks or sometimes a sheltered beach. There was no slip; instead the boat was built where the high spring tides could float it out. No cranes were needed beyond sheerlegs, and axe, adze, brace and caulking hammer were the basic tools. Such boatyards leave little trace but any suitable stretch of bank may be thought a likely site. (The first dry dock was constructed at Portsmouth in 1495.) The Severn estuary saw the construction of a number of galeasses which Henry VIII built for his navy, which combined sails with the oars of a galley. They were not suitable for the rough seas around Britain and were abandoned after the Armada.

The galleon had arrived by then, developed to meet the needs of such worldwide traders as Drake, Hawkins and Frobisher. These kept the high castles of the carracks but were more slender —about four times as long as wide. They were very manoeuvrable and showed their capabilities both in long trading voyages and in battle. They could carry sizeable quantities of cargo and were the basis of the trading companies, such as the East India Company. The company was formed in 1600, when there were only three ships in England of 300 tons or more; by 1615 the company had twelve of over 400 tons, including the *Dragon* of 1,060 and *Hector* of 800. The galleon remained the basic design for overseas trading ships into the eighteenth century, the major changes being a progressive lowering of the castles and the introduction of the steering wheel from 1705. Few ships were built over 1,500 tons, and a boat that size needed about 2,000 oak trees—fifty acres of woodland. Ships this size were too large to be launched and had to be floated out of the yard. Little science went into ship design in Britain at this time. Instead the main guides were long experience, current practice in other countries and some guesswork. The Dutch were the leading ship designers in the sixteenth and seventeenth centuries and their use of labour-saving devices such as wind-powered sawmills kept costs down.

In addition to trading ships there were large numbers of coastal craft. These still included the coracle in the eighteenth century (which can still sometimes be seen on the Severn and in South Wales). Every region had its own craft, which had evolved in response to local needs and waves. The Yorkshire cobble, for example, was almost banana shaped to suit the short, steep waves of the North Sea. By contrast, the Severn trow was a sailing barge which had developed from a raft capable of sliding over the shifting sandbanks. John Appleby of Barton-on-Humber took two men to court in 1533 who had hired his 'Humbre cogge' and sunk it in the river by overloading.

The growing volume of trade in the eighteenth century led to the use of larger river boats of up to 100 tons. This brought the boatmen into conflict with millers using rivers for power. Exeter merchants had already faced this problem when the river had been blocked by a weir, and had constructed a canal past it in 1566. Larger boats frequently grounded in shallow rivers and a number of attempts were made to improve river navigation. Rock outcrops were removed from the river by blasting, pick and shovel; alternatively, halflocks or flashlocks were used to pound up sufficient water to give depth over shallows. The seventeenth century saw schemes to improve river navigation in all parts of England, which were allied with drainage in the East Anglian fens. (The Fossdyke may well have been built by the Romans for drainage but was used by boats between the Trent and the sea in Saxon times.)

Water transport was used wherever possible because of its speed, cheapness and capacity for heavy loads. Since materials did not always originate on a river's banks, tramways were laid down to fill the gap. The earliest known was laid by Huntingdon Beaumont at Wollaton, near Nottingham, in 1603, to carry coal. Another was built in 1605 to take coal from Broseley to the Severn, and there were many such lines by 1650 leading to the staithes in the Tyne. Others carried iron ore, stone and similar bulky goods regularly travelling the same way. The rails were of wood until cheap iron became available in the mid-eighteenth century. The wagons had flanged wheels and were drawn by men or horses on the level, and made use of gravity whenever possible. Such lines were for private use and were not intended to form a network; their sole function was to enable heavy loads to be put on board boat at the nearest point. Water transport was basic to Britain's developing industries in 1750 and it was natural that attempts should be made to develop it still further by the construction of canals. Only later did the advantages of rails become apparent, by which time Britain was in the throes of becoming a full-scale industrial nation.

PLACES TO VISIT

Some of the finest medieval bridges are still standing, such as those at Bideford, Huntingdon and Abingdon, while the Monnow Bridge in Monmouth is the only one to retain its fortified gateway. Wilton Bridge near Ross-on-Wye was built in Elizabethan times, while seventeenth-century coaches can be seen in Nottingham Castle Museum and Cornwall County Museum, Truro. The busier pack routes were paved and many can be traced, especially around Todmorden. There is less to see of shipping but ship models are kept at Buckland Abbey, Plymouth, and many drawings and models at the National Maritime Museum, London. One of the most remarkable remains of the early tramways is the Causey Arch, Tanfield, Co Durham, which was built in 1727.

SECTION C

1750–1970

11 Industrial Acceleration

The upheavals which led to Britain changing from an agricultural country with some industries to an industrial country with some farming are known as the industrial revolution. Opinions still differ widely as to when this revolution began and when it ended, if, indeed, it has ended at all. It is unwise to attach rigid dates to the revolution, for the changes affected most industries but not at the same time. The largest group of changes fell between 1760 and 1800 but the use of coke for smelting iron and the first turnpike roads came half a century earlier and changes that came after 1800 will be seen in later chapters.

'Revolution' suggests a dramatic transformation overnight, which did not happen. 'Acceleration' is nearer the mark but even that did not happen in all industries at the same time. The cotton and iron industries displayed this acceleration best, with new machines and processes making it possible to increase production rapidly. A similar expansion in coal output was brought about with hardly any new methods, while developments in the woollen industry were comparatively slow until it became totally mill-based after 1850. Although the changes were less marked in some industries than others, the expansion of a few industries at the end of the eighteenth century, linked with the use of steam power, made contemporaries aware that the country was rapidly becoming more industrialised. This is what is meant by the term 'industrial revolution'.

One characteristic of the revolution was a change in the organisation of industry. Manufacturing in the home was replaced by full-time work in a factory or mill. The 'jack of all trades' worker gave way to the specialist, and working alongside the employer to a hierarchy of foremen and management. 'We' changed to 'them and us'. Much of the new industrialisation was sited on the coalfields, so that many families were forced to move to new town developments, very different from the neighbourliness of villages. They had to leave behind the small-holding they had combined with their other trade. The migration of people from villages to the towns was in part a consequence of a rapid increase in the population, and also of contemporary developments in agriculture, which allowed sufficient food to be grown to feed the expanding numbers living in towns.

The changes that make up the industrial revolution may be summarised as specialisation; a worker became a specialist in a factory, the factory within its industry and towns within regions. The causes of the revolution were many and varied. It could not have happened in a void; there had to be developments in some industries to lead to expansion in others. Some of these developments were noted in earlier chapters, such as growth in the metal industries or transport improvements. The same was true of regions—the Tamar and upper Trent valleys were areas where industrial development was proceeding faster than elsewhere. Growth in these areas put people in a mood to expect industrial developments, so that they looked for new markets, new machinery, new ways altogether. Improvements in roads and rivers were important for all industries. Growth within an industry focused attention on any process that delayed production and exerted pressures that encouraged the search for a solution, as seen in the cotton industry's search for spinning machines.

More than industrial growth and technical invention was needed to produce a revolution. There had to be a flexible monetary system that could be trusted in all parts of Britain. The formation of the Bank of England in 1694 had helped to stabilise national finances but did little directly to encourage industry outside London. The gap in the provinces was filled by private banks, the first of which was started by a Bristol soap dealer in 1716. Large numbers were founded when trade increased in 1750–3, 1762, 1765–6, 1770–3 and 1789–93, so that there were about 900 private banks in existence by 1815. These issued their own notes and coins—the provision of small change was especially

Page 105
A pair of water-powered
tilt hammers used in a
scythe works. The cogs
(or tappets) press down
the ends of the hammer
shafts, which are pivoted
at the heavy iron castings.
The hammer falls as soon
as the cog passes. The
shears (bottom left) are
driven from the same
shaft.

Page 106 (above) The scythe blades being sharpened on grindstones, also turned by water power; (below) clay crucibles used in the Huntsman steel process. Filled with blister steel, the closed crucibles were lowered into a very hot furnace.

necessary for wages and the markets. Loans obtained from these banks to finance production were vital in bringing about industrialisation within a short time. The availability of money for the banks to borrow to make these loans was also important. Multi-storey mills, for example, cost thousands of pounds to build and equip before they could be used to produce goods that would bring in the money to pay for it all. The fact that there were plentiful supplies of savings which could be borrowed at low rates of interest through the private banks, or more commonly among families, was an important factor in bringing about the industrial revolution.

The same may be said of education. There had to be a bare minimum of education appropriate to industry, and the piecemeal development of schools in the eighteenth century met this requirement. The charity schools and (after 1780) Sunday schools taught reading and writing to those who could attend. The children were therefore able to use printed instructions as machinery became more complex. Education suitable for commerce and merchanting was provided by the dissenting academies and a great array of private schools. The academies were formed from the 1690s, initially to provide education for Nonconformist children who were barred by law from the grammar schools. The education provided was the nearest in England to the quality of the Scots universities. The private schools were of many kinds and were found in all towns. An example from Exeter illustrates the way in which some of them were fitting men for a career in industry—W. Mullings advertised in 1797 that he was opening a school to teach 'Young gentlemen English Grammar, Writing, Arithmetic, Merchants Accounts, Geometry, Land Surveying, Navigation, Geography and Astronomy, with use of the Globes and other branches of Mathematics'. In addition there were a number of itinerant tutors, mostly Scots graduates, who gave lectures on scientific and technical subjects. These and other forms of education were all necessary in speeding the process of industrial change.

Other factors tended to accelerate all these forces in the second half of the eighteenth century. The rate of increase in the population began to rise in the 1750s, and the population continued to grow rapidly into the twentieth century. These extra people both created a demand for more building materials, food, clothing and all other goods and services, and helped to supply them by going to work in the expanding industries. There was also an increasing demand for manufactured goods from overseas after 1785, both from the expanding empire and other countries. Britain had a lead in the large-scale production of manufactured goods which few countries could equal before 1850. The many inventions of this period made possible the production of cheaper goods, and this led to stable and even lower prices since the products of one industry were the raw materials and tools of another.

Travellers and diarists noted the rapid increases in industrial activity towards the end of the century. J. Aiken described events around Manchester in 1795:

> The prodigious extension of the several branches of the Manchester (cotton) manufactures had likewise increased the business of several trades and manufactures connected with or dependent upon them . . . To the ironmongers shops, which are greatly increased of late, are generally annexed smithies, where many articles are made, even to nails. The tin-plate works have found additional employment in furnishing many articles for spinning machines; as have also the braziers in casting wheels for the motion-work of the rollers used in them; and the clock-makers in cutting them. Harness makers have been much employed in making bands for carding engines, and large wheels for the first operation of drawing out the cardings, whereby the consumption of strong curried leather had been much increased.

The rate of acceleration increased further in the first decades of the nineteenth century. The cotton industry had the money to pay for new buildings, which in turn provided more work for builders, engineers and iron producers. An overseas visitor, Christian Beuth, wrote home about the wonders of 1823:

> The modern miracles, my friend, are to me the machines here and the buildings that house them, called factories. Such a block is eight or nine stories high, sometimes has 40 windows along its frontage and is often four windows deep. Each floor is twelve feet high, and vaulted along its whole length with arches each having a span of nine feet. The pillars are of iron, as is the girder which

they support; the side-walls and the enclosing walls are as thin as cards—attaining on the second floor a thickness of less than 2 feet 6 inches. It is said that a storm wrecked one such building in the neighbourhood before it had been completed; that may be true, but a hundred of them are now standing unshaken and exactly as they were erected thirty and forty years ago. A number of such blocks stand in very elevated positions which dominate the neighbourhood; and in addition a forest of even taller boiler house chimneys like needles, so that it is hard to imagine how they remain upright; the whole presents from a distance a wonderful spectacle especially at night, when thousands of windows are brilliantly illuminated by gas-light.

Britain was regarded as 'the workshop of the world' by 1850. This claim was somewhat exaggerated as France and the United States had experienced similar revolutions by then but it underlines the lead Britain had in manufacturing. The industrial growth years of the revolution had seen not merely invention but innovation, which is the widespread use of new inventions by industry. New inventions, whether of machines, methods, raw materials or anything else, have little effect on industry until they are used on a large scale; their innovation brings about the increased production and lower costs. Innovation depends partly on the availability of money for investment and partly on whether industrialists take advantage of the opportunities before them. This leads to another factor in the industrial revolution, the contribution of the Nonconformist churches in shaping character. All the Nonconformist churches stressed the value of hard work, honesty in business and thrift. The law prevented the Dissenters, as they were called, from going to the grammar schools and universities, so they set up their own where the quality of education was far more advanced. Dissenters were banned from most professions, and industry was about the only outlet for their imagination and zeal. The number of manufacturers who were Quakers, for example, was out of all proportion to their numbers. Employers came to prefer Methodists early in the nineteenth century because of their honesty and determination. The Nonconformist attitude to life had a considerable influence on the progress of the revolution.

The acceleration of industrialisation in the eighteenth century was a fusion of all these factors. Some were more influential than others and it would be folly to list them and regard them all as equally important. There were long and short term forces, chance happenings and basic trends, whose cumulative effect was to base Britain's prosperity on what she could manufacture. The changes were not brought about easily. While by 1850 people generally were better off, there were some that were not and many had undergone hardship and misery in the process. Conditions in the mines and factories were a scandal even at the time, and the insanitary state of the industrial towns took years to remedy. Those who worked at home lost their jobs when factory based machines were introduced, and hard learned skills became obsolete the day the factory opened. Levels of pollution and care for the environment were the concern of very few manufacturers, and factory villages like New Lanark developed by David Dale and Robert Owen on the Clyde or Saltaire in Yorkshire built by the mill-owner Titus Salt were very rare even in 1900. While the ultimate effects of the industrial revolution were higher standards of living, industrial advance was not always progress.

The eighteenth-century industrial revolution was based largely on native resources, supplemented by imports. Supplies of iron, coal, wool and building materials met the needs of most industries, and the many streams provided both water and power. The accelerating growth of industry led to increasing imports of all basic raw materials except coal and building materials. Some completely new raw materials were imported in the nineteenth century such as mineral oil, which in time gave rise to entirely new industries (oil-refining, plastics). New sources of power were developed in gas and electricity, and were harnessed by industry at different times. The pace of change in the nineteenth century was such that no firm could adopt all the new developments. Some adopted very few.

The pace of industrial development had become much more piecemeal by 1914. Some industries, such as cotton and coal mining, had expanded fast throughout the nineteenth century, and were paying the price by having large numbers of older machines, mills and methods that could not readily be modernised. Other industries were in a better position. The woollen industry had taken a century to adopt full scale factory methods. Large scale production of steel was relatively new, as were many products of the chemical works. While some of the older industries were stagnating, others were experiencing their own partial revolutions. The major industries no longer experienced expansion at the same time as each other and the events cannot be summarised by one convenient title, though they may be regarded as a continuation of 'industrial acceleration'.

World War I (1914–18) brought a transformation to British industry. Cotton, coal and the railways suffered setbacks from which they never recovered. The war allowed other countries to start their own production and afterwards the British industries could neither catch up nor compete with new factories and forms of transport. By contrast, the motor vehicle industry was given a boost by the war and was able to develop despite the drop in trade and employment in the depression years. The depression was a time of reckoning for those firms that had failed to realise that Britain was no longer the only workshop in the world but had been surpassed by the more modern industries of America, Germany, France and other European countries. In the normal course of events, industries would have faced this fact at different times; the war brought the changes in a few years by taking away Britain's traditional markets and leaving firms to find either new customers or new products. The unemployment and bankruptcies of the depression (1920 to about 1934, though there was still considerable unemployment in 1939) were experienced in all the industrialised countries and were caused by a breakdown in international trade and the monetary system. In Britain these were aggravated by the lack of modernisation that had marked the major industries.

Towards the end of the 1930s and after World War II (1939–45) trade began to grow again on a base of new industries. The growth of electrical engineering and other industries in the 1890s has been called a second industrial revolution, being firmly based on scientific research. Other industries, such as plastics and electronics, developed even later. The pace of industrial development was so hectic that, whereas in the eighteenth century all the major industries expanded within a generation, in the twentieth century industries have developed separately. Their use of electric motors was one thread linking them together, just as the steam engine was central to the growth of all industries after 1775. The importance of power to industry makes it the first topic to be explored in this section.

12 Powerful Steam and Smaller Engines

Increased production depended on power. The heavier machines invented in the eighteenth century could not be worked by hand at home but needed the new factories and their supplies of power. This was water power in most cases, for Newcomen's engine was incapable of turning a wheel directly. The best it could do was to act as a water-returning engine, pumping water from the tail-race of a water wheel back into the mill pond. This arrangement was used at Coalbrookdale in 1742 to drive the furnace bellows, and in a number of other places. There was no need for such arrangements in places where there was an adequate water supply and few firms used it, and water wheels continued to be installed and worked for many years. A twenty-seven-foot dia-meter wheel was set up at Holford Combe, Somerset, for example, in 1893, and was used successively for crushing rock, pumping water, sawing wood and grinding bark, and finally to generate electricity. Industrialists saw little need to install expen-sive engines or motors if their power needs could be met by water, which continued to be used into the twentieth century. Wind power was also used, mainly for grinding flour and pump-ing water. The need for power outstripped the possible supplies of wind and water power in most areas, and only the develop-ment of the steam engine made expansion possible.

STEAM

The atmospheric engine designed by Thomas Newcomen early in the eighteenth century was adequate for draining mines, and simple to erect and operate. The parts could be made by local smiths and assembled on site, though there were marked variations in the quality of the resulting engines, and therefore in their efficiency. John Smeaton made careful inquiries into some of these engines in the 1760s, and incorporated a number of improvements in the design of engines he erected himself. In particular he was able to have cylinders made with a truly round bore by the Carron Ironworks in Scotland which began work in 1760. The improvements doubled the efficiency of the engine and made the fullest use of the technology of the day. However, the engine remained a pumping engine, and attempts to convert it to rotary motion were regarded as pointless by Smeaton and other engineers. When in the 1780s some Newcomen engines were adapted for rotary working they were found to be slow and jerky, compared to the smooth running of water wheels.

Another engineer, James Watt, was also at work on the shortcomings of the atmospheric engine in the 1760s. He was a friend of Smeaton but went much further in his research and inventions. His knowledge of the theories of latent heat put forward by Dr Black in 1764 led him to realise the need for removing the condensing of steam from the cylinder. Much of the inefficiency of the atmospheric engine was due to the continual heating of the cylinder to hold steam for the power stroke, followed by cooling it to condense the steam. The heating-cooling cycle also wasted much fuel. Watt proposed in 1765 that the steam should be condensed in a condenser outside the cylinder, so that the cylinder could be kept hot while the condenser could be immersed in a tank of cold water.

Watt went into partnership with John Roebuck of the Carron Ironworks in 1768, and they patented the new form of engine in 1769. A trial engine was made but would not work and all attempts to improve it failed. The fault lay not in the idea but in the limited technology available. Both men fell into debt and Watt was tempted to abandon his ideas as impracticable. This was prevented by Matthew Boulton, the owner of an ironworks in Soho, Birmingham. Boulton took over Roebuck's share of the partnership, Watt moved to Soho in 1774 and the new firm of Boulton and Watt renewed the patent the following year. John

Wilkinson had installed a cannon boring lathe at his Bersham works in 1774 and a new cylinder was cut on it. The bore was not only circular but the sides were parallel, a marked improvement on the Carron cylinder. The new cylinder and other parts were assembled in 1775, and the engine worked.

Boulton and Watt produced engines commercially from 1776 and the engines were popular despite the initial cost. Fuel consumption was halved, which was most important to all users except the coal mines who used the slack that could not be sold. Forty engines were erected in Cornwall alone in 1777–88, where the lack of any coal nearer than South Wales made the new engines most attractive. The engine was still a pumping (reciprocating) engine, and was mainly used in the copper mines which had been closing down for lack of an economic form of drainage.

Many more potential users took notice in 1781 when Watt produced an engine capable of rotary motion. The beam was harnessed to a large flywheel by the cumbersome sun and planet gears designed by William Murdoch, another Scot working for Boulton and Watt. (This arrangement was replaced by a straightforward crank in 1794.) The availability of an engine that could drive machinery directly opened the way to the widespread use of machines that had only been used in a few places up to this time. Cotton and worsted mills, pottery firms and sugar refiners had steam engines by 1800, as did maltsters, brewers and millers. Watt did not stop there but added one improvement after another. The double-acting engine came in 1782, abandoning atmospheric pressure. Parallel motion (1784) made it possible for the piston rod to push as well as pull, while the governor, adapted from water wheel practice in 1788, allowed the speed of the engine to be controlled.

The result of all these improvements to the basic Newcomen engine was to transform an inefficient, costly pumping engine into an economical and adaptable source of power. While many processes could and would continue to be done by water power and by hand, there were many that had been held back by the lack of sufficient power. Boulton and Watt supplied it in a range of engines to meet all requirements. On these engines, and those of imitators like Fenton, Murray & Co of Leeds, was based the mass production of cotton cloth and cheap clothes, of cheaper iron, of an extending range of engineering products and supplies of water to the industrial towns. The transformation of transport was soon to be added to these, when Richard Trevithick devised the high-pressure boiler. The possibilities created by the variety of engines now available were welcomed by industrialists. Many of them set up mills and foundries on the coalfields, within easy reach of fuel. This led to the migration of very many families from rural areas to rapidly expanding, smoke-laden towns. Many kinds of power were to follow in the nineteenth century, from massive compound steam engines to small electric motors. None was so marked a change from existing sources of power as Watt's engines, or brought about so many changes in society. Compared to the strongest source available, water wheels, the steam engine was more powerful, independent of stream levels, capable of running at constant speeds and able to be set up anywhere. It was not surprising that industrialists were quick to install such engines, or that many industries were transformed as a result.

This new industrial activity was in addition to the existing mills and factories. As noted before, many industrialists were satisfied with the performance of water wheels. A Manchester cotton spinner, Mr Henshall, in 1847 worked out the annual running costs of a 100hp steam engine to be £416, and of a 100hp water wheel to be £107 7s (£107.35). Some manufacturers used both. In 1809 a Lancashire cotton bleacher used a water wheel 18ft diameter and 15ft wide in the winter months when water was plentiful but coal difficult to move over muddy roads. In the summer, when the reverse was true, he used a 5hp engine. The steam engine made work possible all the year round, providing full-time employment and increased production. In this, and in totally new ways later, the steam engine was the agent of change in those industries that had machines to drive.

The use of steam for transport is covered more fully in chapter 18. It included the use of beam engines to pump water into the summit levels of canals, the development of the steam locomotive for rails and roads and the slower adoption of engines in ships. Transport before this had been confined to the speed of a horse; the steam engine introduced ever increasing speeds at lower costs.

The horizontal mill engine had been developed by 1870 and was increasingly used wherever power was needed throughout a factory. Endless ropes passed from the flywheel to each floor of the factory. The ropes drove overhead shafting running the length of the factory, and a belt was brought down to each machine. In this way the one steam engine drove machinery on many floors. Mill engines were at first single cylinder but after 1854 two-cylinder compound engines were available. This engine was designed by John Elder and made use of the fact that steam expands. The steam was first admitted to a high-pressure cylinder, and from there to a larger low-pressure cylinder. Fuel consumption was cut by a third, which made compound engines particularly attractive to shipbuilders. Large numbers of steam engines, compound and single-cylinder, beam and horizontal, were installed in mills, factories and foundries all over the country after 1850. These made it possible for England to be the workshop of the world but also meant that few industrialists wanted to replace expensive engines with newer forms of power as these were developed.

GAS AND OIL ENGINES

Steam and gas engines had a common ancestry, for the Dutch scientist Christian Huygens tried to use gunpowder to move a piston within a cylinder before turning his attention to steam. The future clearly lay with steam and, although Isambard Brunel and others experimented with 'gaz' engines early in the nineteenth century, the first working gas engine of any note did not appear until 1859. This was designed by the Frenchman Etienne Lenoir but its performance did not equal that of a comparable steam engine. In 1876 N. A. Otto produced the horizontal engine based on a four-stroke cycle which became the normal pattern within a few years. The Otto cycle was also used in oil engines. The explosive gas was drawn in on the first stroke and compressed and ignited on the second. The explosion drove the piston back to make the third stroke and the waste gases were driven out on the fourth.

The gas engine met a need for a small source of power at the end of the nineteenth century. The German firm of Otto and

Langen made 50,000 gas engines, 1876-83, of which the great majority were between one and three horsepower. A number of British makers, such as Bates of Manchester or Rustons of Lincoln, were soon making engines, and they were in widest use about 1920. The size of some had increased to 5,000hp by this time, for use in pumping stations, but most were still small. They ran on town gas from the gasworks and were stationary engines. They were used wherever power demands were light or irregular—in saw mills and joiners shops, blacksmiths, oil blenders, printers and similar situations. They supplied power more cheaply than if a steam engine and boiler had been used.

Gas engines were restricted to towns by the limits of the piped supply. Oil engines were free of such restrictions, for the fuel could be transported, stored and fed to the engine by gravity. The petroleum industry was able to supply oils and petrol in any quantity, and a number of firms found the oil engine useful for small power requirements.

The first successful oil engine was patented by Akroyd Stuart in 1890, who sold one horsepower engines for £90 and ten horsepower models for £270 from his small works in Bletchley. Part of his advertising read:

> One penny per horse power per hour . . . It possesses all the advantages of the most modern gas engines, and, in addition, it is independent of a local gas supply. It is not only designed for stationary purposes, but may be built as Portable, Launch, Traction, Tramcar or Fire Engines, in fact the motive power is so portable that it may be used anywhere.

The engine ran on paraffin and was made by the Grantham firm of Hornsby from 1892, five years before Rudolf Diesel produced a similar engine which gave his name to all oil engines. Hornsbys built up a commanding lead in the production of these engines, which led to a significant export trade. The engines were increasingly used in the twentieth century to generate electricity in areas remote from a mains supply.

ELECTRIC MOTORS

Michael Faraday demonstrated the principle of the electric

motor in 1831 but many years passed before it was put to practical use. The delay was due in part to the fact that manufacturers were only just beginning to install steam engines. Far more serious was the complete absence of electricity generating stations, and they would only be built when there was a demand for electricity. This began to grow in the 1870s with the use of electric lighting. Holborn Viaduct generating station began in 1882 and was soon joined by others. Most used coal-fired steam engines to drive generators, but Charles Parsons's efficient steam turbines were used in the North-East while the boilers in Nottingham were fed with town refuse.

Electricity held little appeal for manufacturers in the nineteenth century. Steam engines and overhead shafting were still at the height of their popularity, while gas and oil engines were being developed at the same time, also for use with shafting. The idea of having individual electric motors for each machine was too novel, and most manufacturers were against the idea. Only in the North-East, where Sir Charles Parsons was a lively propagandist for the new form of power, were motors at all common before 1900. They tended to be used in the small workshops, by joiners, tailors, shoe-repairers and other low-power users. Early in the twentieth century some textile mills installed their own generating plant, either using their existing steam engine or installing a turbine. They could then conserve power and only run those machines that were needed, for the great advantage of electric motors was that each machine was now independently powered instead of a single engine turning all the line shafting at once.

Some Yorkshire mills abandoned their water wheels in the 1950s and installed water-turbines driven from the mill pond, so generating electricity for motors. In doing so they were reflecting the widespread adoption of motors in industry after 1918. This was particularly noticeable in such new industries as the production of cars and aircraft, which had no money invested in older forms of power. Other industries also adopted the motor, for its flexibility and cleanliness made for easier working conditions. One side effect of the use of electricity was a slow movement of industry away from the coalfields to the towns around London.

This gave them access to raw materials and markets, and more pleasant surroundings. By 1960 very few windmills, water wheels, steam and gas engines remained in use, oil engines were seldom used except in large units for pumping or electricity generating, and the electric motor was the principal power source in all industries. In this respect the motor had brought about a complete change in power use in less than eighty years, though the impact of the change was less marked than the introduction of the steam engine had been early in the nineteenth century.

TURBINES AND JETS

The steam turbine already mentioned was patented by Sir Charles Parsons in 1884. He designed it specifically to generate electricity and made some capable of 1,000kW in 1893. He also tried to interest the Admiralty in turbines and, when they took no notice, caused them considerable embarrassment by driving a turbine-powered boat, the *Turbinia*, in and out of the ships arranged for the Jubilee Naval Review in 1897 at $34\frac{1}{2}$ knots. No naval ship could manage much more than half that speed; the navy was using marine turbines by 1907.

The jet engine, designed by Frank Whittle in 1937, and the gas turbine developed in 1950 have had few applications outside transport. They are large units, for which there is little need in industry when the individual electric motor can be made so adaptable. Each development of sources of power gave rise to new industries producing the power units, and also making other machines to be driven by them. They also required substantial supplies of raw materials, particularly coal.

PLACES TO VISIT

A post mill has been re-erected at the Avoncroft Museum of Buildings, Stoke Prior, Worcestershire, and another is in the care of the Department for the Environment at Saxtead Green, Suffolk. External water wheels can be seen in many places. The one at Preston Mill, East Linton, East Lothian, is still connected to its grinding machinery and is in working order, and the giant Laxey Wheel in the Isle of Man has been restored. A water pressure beam engine is preserved at Wanlockhead, Dumfries, Cornish engines in Camborne and Redruth, and later pumping engines in Coleham Pumping Station, Shrewsbury. The Birmingham Museum of Science and Industry is one of the few places where a gas engine may be seen but the most comprehensive display of power sources is in the Science Museum, London.

13   Deeper Mines and New Sites

Statistics are nowadays collected about everything imaginable, a custom that accelerated in the mid-nineteenth century. Figures before that time are frequently sketchy or non-existent and can seldom be relied on in full. It is estimated that the production of coal in England and Wales was $2\frac{1}{2}$ million tons in 1700, and that this increased to ten million tons by 1800 when Scotland's output was included. Coal production was particularly important in Northumberland and Durham, and more detailed figures exist of shipments of coal from Newcastle and Sunderland. These give some indication of the periods in which output increased:

Average annual shipments per decade	
1750s	1,237,550
1760s	1,366,400
1770s	figures missing
1780s	1,611,200
1790s	2,000,750
1800s	2,334,650
1810s	2,766,600
1820s	3,368,150

The increasing amount each decade by which the figures grow is an indication of economic growth. Coal was used as a source of heat in many industries in the eighteenth century, for example in soap boiling, sugar refining, brewing, brick making and the metal industries. Watt's development of the steam engine led to a marked increase in coal consumption.

Page *123* (*above*) Mass production, as seen in a tractor works. The parts have been selected from bins and brought to one place, where they are assembled. The tractor in the shadows is nearly complete; (*below*) the same factory some years later, where flow line methods have been introduced. The developing tractor is moved continuously from one end to the other, and the mechanics add the same components to each as it passes.

Page 124 Developments in the engineering of consumer goods are illustrated in these three electric cookers, which were made in 1919 (*above left*), 1926 (*above right*) and 1945 (*left*).

Coal was mined in other areas than the North-East by 1800. Yorkshire, Lancashire, Derbyshire, Leicestershire, Warwickshire, Nottinghamshire, Staffordshire, South Wales, Ayrshire and the Scottish Lowlands were the main areas of production. Coal was also mined less extensively in other counties, such as the scattered workings in Somerset and Gloucestershire, or the later development of the Kent coalfield.

The demand for coal increased steadily to 1913. A larger population needed more coal for domestic fires and cooking. The demands of industry were even greater. Steam engines in industry and the railways consumed increased quantities, and both gas and electricity were produced from coal in this period. Coal was also becoming a raw material in the chemical industry for the production of tar and many synthetic materials. Figures are more plentiful to illustrate the growth of coal output after 1850, and may be seen in Fig 16. In 1913 287 million tons were mined, the highest total ever reached, and ninety-eight million tons of this were exported, mostly to European countries. The export trade stopped during World War I and never recovered

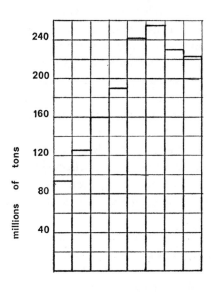

1860s — 1930s

Fig 16 *Average annual output of coal per decade*

afterwards because of the marked increase in coal production in Europe during the war. The need for coal for raising steam was being replaced by oil and gas, gas and electricity were used to make steel, and all three were being used in the home. (Less coal was needed to make gas or electricity than if coal had been used direct on a fire or with a steam engine.) The coal industry therefore began an uneven contraction which continued to 1970.

The loss of the export trade and the success of coal's competitors were probably inevitable. The contraction in the industry that they brought about was made more certain by the manner in which the industry had been allowed to develop, with no clear eye to the future. Most pits in the eighteenth century were small, employing twenty men, women and children, though some were larger. A few pits in the North-East had shafts 200ft deep but the majority of pits were shallow, and many adit mines and bell pits were still being worked. Coal was mined with pickaxes and shovelled into baskets which were wound to the surface in the smaller pits or carried up a succession of ladders by women in the deeper mines. The marked growth of the industry to 1913 was brought about by employing more people with more picks and shovels. A few minor improvements were introduced but there was no revolutionary change in method or mechanisation. There was no new innovation in the coal industry and production was determined by the numbers of people employed. Fig 17 shows the increase in employment within the industry, and the shape of the graph is identical to that of coal production until the 1920s. A number of prolonged strikes accelerated the fall in coal production in that decade, and the introduction of coal cutting and other machines is reflected in the fall in employment in the 1930s, when production per man was increasing. The reduction in the numbers in the industry also continued to 1970.

All coal pits in the eighteenth century were privately owned, whether it was a single pit by a free miner in the Forest of Dean or the vast numbers on the northern estates of the 'Grand Allies', Lord Wharncliffe, Lord Ravensworth and the Earl of Strathmore. A clear example of the way some landowners developed the mines on their estates can be seen in the canal built by the Duke

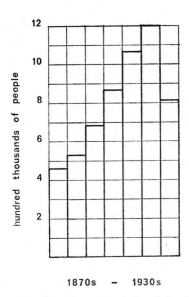

Fig 17 *Average annual employment per decade in the coal industry*

of Bridgewater to take coal to Manchester. As the demand for coal increased shafts were made deeper and galleries extended further from the shafts. This posed drainage problems, which were overcome by hand pumps, rag pumps powered by men, horses or water wheels, and Newcomen engines (more than 100 were at work in the North-East in 1770). Mines became deeper with every advance in drainage. Another problem was the danger of explosion from pockets of methane and other gases in the galleries. Candles were the only light available until 1815 and caused many disasters. Safety lamps were perfected in 1815 by George Stephenson and Sir Humphrey Davy, and reduced the number of explosions. The number of deaths and injuries did not decrease, however, for the lamps encouraged owners to open up more dangerous shafts and levels, and accidents caused by rock falls, cave-ins and other disasters continued. An explosion at Oaks Colliery near Barnsley in Yorkshire killed 361 men and boys in 1866. While this was horrifying enough, a further 2,000 people had been killed in the same colliery in the previous fifty years, and this appalling accident rate was all too common. Mining was a dangerous job and miners tended to live wild lives in consequence. John Wesley's first concern had been the miners near Bristol, who were neglected by everyone else. They were better off than workers in the Scottish mines and salt pits, who were treated like serfs; they had to work in the same mine for life, and were sold with the mine. This practice was abolished by Acts in 1775 and 1799. Conditions in other mines were brutal in the first half of the nineteenth century, with children hauling tubs along rails on their hands and knees, or sitting in the dark closing a door to keep the air circulating. The Mines Act of 1842 banned women and children under ten from working underground but many were employed to sort coal and attend to other surface jobs, while an eighteen-hour day for eleven year olds was still legal.

The movement of miners in shafts became safer with the use of wire cables, introduced from Germany about 1850. This allowed wire cages to be lowered, in place of ladders, and the tubs of coal were brought out the same way. Winding engines and the familiar headstock wheels were set up, and ponies were used underground in the larger mines.

Increased production towards the end of the nineteenth century was brought about by sinking new shafts and working narrower seams. Coal was expensive to mine from such pits but there was no lack of customers before 1913. Coal cutters, conveyor belts below and above ground, mechanical sorting and many other aids were well-known in American pits at this time but only a handful of colliery owners installed them in Britain, others continuing to employ more men with more picks and shovels. The depressed state of trade after 1919, both at home and overseas, left the mine owners stranded. Coal from pits that were expensive to work would not sell, and no capital had been put aside for mechanisation or marketing. Many of the seams being worked could not have been mechanised at all but nothing had been done to develop new ones. It was as if the colliery owners had thought that coal would always be bought, no matter how expensive; lack of competition from other fuels had made them shortsighted in the way they ran the industry. Relations between miners and managers were bad and became bitter leading to strikes in the 1920s; 41 per cent of coal workers were unemployed in the summer of 1932, because so little coal was being sold. Many remedies were suggested. Amalgamations of mines and joint selling agencies were tried but found ineffective. The mines had been government controlled for part of the war, and the Sankey Commission recommended in 1919 that they should be nationalised, so that a national plan could be drawn up for the first time, uneconomic pits closed and the rest modernised. The advice was ignored and the pits were returned to their owners, mostly in a run-down state. They were state controlled again from 1938, and were finally nationalised in 1947. The many private owners were compensated, and the National Coal Board faced the problems of modernising a run-down industry in the face of competition from the 'clean' fuels, electricity and oil.

GAS, ELECTRICITY AND OIL

The process of extracting gas from coal was discovered by William Murdoch while he was supervising the erection of Boulton and Watt's engines in Cornwall in 1792. His employers were impressed, built their own gas retorts and holder, and lit the Soho works by gas in about 1800. Later they sold apparatus for a while—a Salford mill was lit by 900 of their gas lights in 1807. However, gas lighting was not popular because of the unpleasant smell, and the firm ceased production in 1814.

Two years earlier, the Gas Light and Coke Company began in London, and had laid twenty-six miles of cast iron gas main by 1816. The gas was produced in iron retorts and was then cooled, purified with lime and washed. These processes removed some of the smell. Other producing companies began, so that fifty-two English towns had some gas lighting in 1823 and 1,000 gas works had been set up by 1859. Some of these were in factory yards, and any surplus gas was supplied to nearby houses. For most of the century the lights were open flames which were dim, smoky, noisy and hot, and only slightly preferable to whale oil lamps. The burners were mounted on the wall or suspended from the ceiling. The coming of electric light stimulated research leading to the invention in 1885 of the incandescent mantle, which gave a much better light.

Other gas appliances were accepted at intervals. Single rings for cooking and geysers for heating water were available in the 1860s, and cooking by gas had increased significantly by the seventies. Fires were not widely used until after 1900. The manufacture of these appliances formed a growing branch of the iron and steel industry.

The use of gas for motive power was noted in the previous chapter, and industry used it in other ways. Some potteries adopted it to fire kilns in 1855 and Siemens used it for steel conversion in 1866. Other firms changed to gas when their processes were modernised, particularly in the 1930s. By then the use of liquid petroleum gas (LPG) was being investigated. This was at that time a waste product of the oil refineries and therefore cheaper than town gas made from coal. It became more popular after 1945 and 30,000 tons were used in 1950. Its use then grew rapidly to 1·2 million tons in 1968, by which time it was being deliberately made at oil refineries. It was used by some gas boards in place of town gas, by the steel industry for cutting metals, and by glass and ceramics firms to fire kilns, while the distinctive cylinders carried by campers and caravanners became well known. It was easy to transport, needed no supply pipes and was clean to handle and burn.

The history of natural gas in Britain is even more recent, though it had been used in America almost from the start of the oil industry. The search for it in Europe began in 1959 with the discovery of the Dutch field in Slochteren. The major oil companies spent £10 million on research, 1963–5, leading to the worthwhile fields found by *Sea Gem* in 1965. A further £100 million was spent in the next two years to find the extent of the fields, and pipelines began to be laid. Plans were made almost at once to convert Britain's millions of appliances to use natural gas in preference to town gas or LPG, and the long programme of conversion began in 1967.

Compared with these, the history of electricity generation is quite lengthy. Research into the nature and measurement of electricity was an international matter in the eighteenth century, carried out by such individuals as Volta, Ampere and Benjamin Franklin. The body of knowledge was used by Michael Faraday to demonstrate the principles of a generator and motor in 1831.

Little was done with the knowledge as there was little interest in electricity as a source of power and no other apparatus that could use it. The use of electric arc lights in lighthouses from 1858 paved the way for further development, and the filament light bulb using cotton thread or bamboo as the filament in a vacuum bulb was developed independently by Joseph Swan in Britain and Thomas Edison in America. They combined in 1883. Tungsten was the normal filament by 1911. The Holborn Viaduct generating station began in London in 1882 and the use of electricity began to accelerate from that time. Some towns established their own stations as a local government service and, as well as supplying private consumers, used electricity to run trams. Other towns had cheap gas lighting and were in no more hurry than industry generally to switch to electricity. Gradually the electrical industry grew, spurred on by electrical engineers from abroad. Alexander Siemens started works at Stafford, Sebastian de Ferranti made meters, transformers and large generators, while the American George Westinghouse started his works at Trafford Park, Manchester, in 1899. They and smaller firms created the electrical engineering industry, which was making fires and cookers in the 1920s, expensive refrigerators and vacuum cleaners by 1939 and fluorescent lights in 1940. The development of the industry during and after World War II made these items increasingly common by 1960, as well as electric drills, washing-machines, food mixers, radio and television, and discharge lamps such as neon signs and sodium street lights. The application of individual motors to machines transformed many firms by allowing them to arrange machines to enable flow production methods to be used. The use of electricity in industry increased rapidly in the 1920s, especially after the Central Electricity Generating Board was set up in 1926. The Board closed a few of the smaller and less economic generating stations, and built a hundred much larger ones. It also created the national grid of power lines, to balance the output of the power stations with the varying needs of consumers. The use of atomic energy to produce electricity began with the opening of the Calder Hall reactor in 1956, where heat from the reaction made steam to drive turbines. This was followed by the first fast reactor at Dounreay in 1959 and other power stations after that. The contribution of these stations to the national grid grew by 1970, though not as fast as some had predicted.

The oil industry, by contrast, developed steadily before the introduction of internal combustion engines, and faster afterwards. Oil shales outcrop in many parts of Britain, and the beds in the Lothians and Fife were rich and accessible enough to be worked from 1850 by James Young. The industry grew rapidly and mined 2½ million tons from the area in 1905. The shale was heated and oil was given off as a vapour. This was condensed and refined to give petrol, paraffin wax, lubricating oils and tar. Although the Scottish oil industry was still in existence in 1950, home production had for long been surpassed by the arrival of oil tankers from America and the Persian Gulf, which began shipments in 1885. This led to the establishment of refineries at ports like Southampton where large tankers could dock. The oil was refined to make fuels for transport and was the raw material for some industries, such as plastics.

ORE EXTRACTION

The industrial revolution caused continual increases in the demand for metals, especially iron. This had been mined in several districts for centuries, and other areas were developed. Production figures exist from 1855 and the following table gives the main regions and output at ten-year intervals:

				Leics Northants Rutland Oxfords	Cumberland & Lancs	Staffs Shrops & Worcs	Scotland
	Total	Cleveland	Lincolnshire				
1855	9,554	865	—	74	538	1,221	2,400
1865	9,910	2,762	125	364	1,504	1,759	1,470
1875	15,821	6,122	573	1,086	1,982	1,895	2,452
1885	15,418	5,932	1,189	1,471	2,438	2,039	1,838
1895	12,615	5,286	1,544	1,751	2,013	916	825
1905	14,591	5,944	2,151	2,851	1,639	912	832
1915	14,235	4,746	3,149	3,343	1,656	707	375
1925	10,143	2,284	2,498	3,967	952	288	14
1935	10,895	1,640	3,449	4,652	840	151	39

Output of iron ore in Britain in thousands of tons

Imports of iron ore fluctuated around five million tons a year from 1885–1920, then declined. The industry continued to meet the bulk of British requirements to 1970.

This was not so with the non-ferrous metals. The Cornish tin mines were able to increase production with the aid of the Watt steam engines. The veins were narrow and mining was difficult but production averaged 14,000 tons a year from 1860–90. Imports of much cheaper tin from Malaysia made the mines increasingly uneconomic and one after another shut down from the 1930s onwards.

Copper mining began in Cornwall in the eighteenth century and reached its greatest extent in the 1850s. Copper was also being mined in the Isle of Man by then, and exploitation of Anglesey copper took place from 1770–1840. Cornish miners worked an eight-hour shift, even in the eighteenth century, and work was continuous from Monday to Saturday. Water wheels and gins were used to raise the ore, it was crushed by heavy wooden stamps driven by water power and sorted by women before being smelted. Imports were again the cause of decline, and production fell from 361,300 tons of ore in 1856 to 36,200 in 1885.

Steam drainage had been used in Cornwall and was also used in lead mines in Flintshire and Cardiganshire, in north Yorkshire and Derbyshire, while the mighty Laxey wheel drained some Manx mines. The general picture of difficult and consequently expensive mining was evident in lead mining too and, after a boom in the industry from 1840–70, cheaper imports led to a slow decline afterwards. Some lead was recovered from the Roman slag tips by the process of buddling. The slag was crushed and carried in water to a point where it would pour into the centre of a shallow, circular pit. The heavy lead sank to the bottom in the middle, while lighter material was carried to the edges. A cone built up and, when the water had drained away, the lead fragments were dug from the middle of the cone and the rest discarded. The lead was smelted again to produce molten lead suitable for casting. It became uneconomic to continue working this slag after 1907. A brief revival in the 1930s, mainly in Derbyshire, was followed by the virtual extinction of lead mining in Britain. Some interest was shown in prospecting for new veins of these three metals in the 1960s but the cost of mining the British ores proved prohibitive at that time.

PLACES TO VISIT

Mining sometimes scars the landscape, at other times leaves little trace on the surface. In either case, little can be learned from visiting former mining areas. As old mine workings can be very dangerous, they are best viewed from a distance. There are remains of ore processing near many mining areas, such as the lead buddles in the Mendips and the smelt mills in the Yorkshire dales. An interesting collection of lead mining tools is kept in the castle at Castle Bolton, Yorkshire, and a display illustrating aluminium processing can be seen in the West Highland Museum, Fort William, Inverness. Coal mining is shown in the Science Museum, London, the museum of the Department of Mining Engineering, Newcastle upon Tyne, and the Lound Hall Mining Museum, Retford, Nottinghamshire.

14 Metals Make Machines

Where wool and cloth characterised British industry in the Middle Ages, the metal trades increasingly came to dominate the scene in the eighteenth century. The beginnings of expansion in the iron industry have already been noted in the use of coke for smelting that Abraham Darby developed in 1709. This led to a rapid growth in the volume of work done in his foundries around Coalbrookdale, and to a growth in the industry as a whole when the secret of his success leaked out in 1740. The iron produced by Darby's process was used for casting firebacks and other household goods. The iron was unsuitable for forging into wrought iron until Abraham Darby II added limestone to the blast furnace, which removed some impurities. However, it took twelve hours to make a ton of wrought iron in a finery from pigs of coke-smelted iron. Wrought iron could be hammered into sheets, girders and rods, and the sheets slit into strips for the nail-makers. This was the only way to make wrought iron until 1783, and in addition the whole industry was handicapped by poor transport and lack of power.

Steel making had been very difficult and costly, and was reserved for the more expensive knives, swords and edge tools. It had never been possible to make bars of steel, which had had to be imported from Sweden by the jewellers and clockmakers who needed them. Benjamin Huntsman perfected a way of making steel about 1740, which involved heating iron and charcoal in closed crucibles for long periods. The steel was of excellent quality and was welcomed by the makers of clock springs and high-class cutlery. It was very expensive, however, and the widespread use of steel had to await mass production processes.

135

The users of iron and steel were widely scattered, largely because of the lack of adequate transport. Iron ingots were difficult enough to move about because of their weight but iron goods were bulky as well. Castings weighing several tons could well take months to travel a hundred miles. Iron founders could only overcome the problem by having ingots brought to suitable sites near customers, and making the castings there. The craftsmen needing steel were highly specialised, and were to be found in most large towns, in particular Sheffield. That town also made all kinds of iron tools, while Birmingham was noted for its trinket makers and gunsmiths. Customers out of reach of these towns were dependent on the capabilities of a village blacksmith. Increasing production of iron after 1750 was to lead to many more specialists and to the formation of engineering firms.

IRON

The Weald of Sussex declined as an iron mining area in the seventeenth century, and most of the Forest of Dean mines were exhausted in the eighteenth. Instead the industry expanded on the coalfields in Shropshire and the Black Country, South Wales, south Yorkshire and the Scottish Lowlands, where coal and iron ore were readily accessible. Figures only exist for the amount of pig iron produced, and these show a growth from an estimated 25,000 tons in 1720 to 125,000 tons in 1796 and 2,700,000 in 1852. Whereas the amount of iron imported in 1720 (23,600 tons) was nearly as great as home production, imports did not begin to rise appreciably until the 1860s, though the amount fluctuated widely from year to year. (Imports of iron ore did not become significant until 1870. The Cleveland mines were being developed rapidly by that time, and mines in Lincolnshire were beginning to produce significant amounts.)

The increasing demand for iron came from several directions. Enterprising manufacturers found new uses for cast iron in the eighteenth century. The Darbys, for example, made steam engine cylinders and cast-iron rails for their network of tramways in 1767, and Abraham Darby III made the castings and supervised the erection of the first bridge made of iron at Ironbridge in 1779. 'Iron mad' John Wilkinson had works nearby and was a born publicist. He built an iron barge, the *Trial*, in 1787 for use on the Severn, supplied water pipes to Paris and cannon to both France and England. The lathe he designed for boring the cannon brought him orders for steam-engine cylinders from Boulton and Watt. Many new machines were being invented in other industries by this time, which would have been better if they could have been made of iron. The lack of a way of making wrought iron cheaply made this impossible, apart from those items which could be cast.

Cast iron contained carbon which was removed by forging, leaving wrought iron. Several men looked for ways of making larger quantities at a time, and it was Henry Cort that found the answer in 1783. He adapted a blast furnace so that the molten iron could be stirred while the air was forced through it, allowing the carbon to burn away. The following year he adapted existing rolling mills so that loops of iron could be taken from the puddling furnace, as it was called, and rolled into sheets, bars or girders as required without having to be reheated. The new process made fifteen tons of wrought iron an hour, ready rolled, which was a far cry from the best that could be done even by the Darbys. Wrought iron became immediately cheaper, and many new firms began to exploit the puddling process. The three largest ironworks in 1806 were all in South Wales, at Cyfarthfa, Pen y daren and Blaenavon. Cort's process finally ended the industry's dependence on charcoal and made rapid expansion possible.

The cheapness of iron also attracted new customers. It was now reasonable to make iron-framed machines, which in turn required the development of machine tools. Iron-framed buildings began with cotton mills, where there was an urgent need for fireproof construction. In 1828 John Neilson began to use a hot blast in the furnace in place of the cold blast that had been used in all furnaces before. The advantage was that coal could be used without being coked, cutting fuel consumption by half. Pig iron producers were then set fair for a prosperous thirty years, with demands from many customers, including the new railways, continually growing.

Steel is a compound of iron and a small amount of carbon, and is stronger than iron. The first successful process for making steel in bulk was devised by Henry Bessemer in 1856. Molten pig iron was poured into a cylindrical furnace (called a convertor) and a hot blast was driven through to remove impurities, particularly carbon and silicon. A measured amount of carbon was added towards the end of the blast and the steel was ready for rolling. The kind of steel made was mild steel and, though scorned by Sheffield cutlers because it could not keep a cutting edge, it was welcomed by the railways who needed stronger rails that would last longer than iron.

Ten years later, William Siemens invented the open hearth process of making mild steel. The iron was spread over a larger area in a reverberatory furnace, where the hot blast passed over the surface instead of through the iron. The process took longer but this allowed greater control over the quality of each batch. Firms using the open hearth competed with those who had installed convertors, which resulted in low steel prices and the rapid use of steel in place of iron. This did not mean a decline in the iron industry, since iron was needed to make the steel, but less iron was used as the finished product.

Neither of the processes, known as the acid processes, could use iron containing phosphorus, which all British ores did except those mined in Cumberland. Iron had to be imported from Sweden and Spain for conversion to steel until S. G. Thomas and Percy Gilchrist found that phosphorus combined with limestone to form basic slag (which could be ground down for fertiliser). Phosphoric ores could be used if the base lining of the furnaces was made of limestone, which gave rise to the name basic process whether limestone was used in convertors or open hearths. The idea was demonstrated in 1879, and was soon used in Britain. Germany, America and other countries made even faster use of it as they had larger reserves of phosphoric ores. The changing popularity of the different processes is illustrated in the following chart of steel production, 1871-1931:

Year	Total	Bessemer		Open hearth	
	Thousands of tons	Acid process	Basic process	Acid process	Basic process
1871	329	329		—	
1881	1,778	1,440		338	
1891	3,157	1,306	336	1,415	100
1901	4,904	1,116	491	2,946	351
1911	6,462	888	573	3,131	1,869
1921	3,703	209	54	1,170	2,217
1931	5,203	129	—	1,182	3,785

Seventy-six per cent of steel in 1963 was made on basic open hearths, while electric furnaces, which Siemens had first used in 1879, only accounted for 9·5 per cent.

MACHINE TOOLS

Boulton was delighted that Wilkinson could bore a fifty-inch cylinder for him that 'doth not err the thickness of an old shilling in no part'. Lack of accuracy had prevented Watt's engine from working, and no improvement was possible until machines were invented that could shape metals to within thousandths of an inch of what was required. Once machines were available it was possible to make any number of the same item, each identical to the others.

For lack of such machines in the eighteenth century most machinery had wooden frames and only the working parts were metal. The frames were made very heavy in an attempt to prevent warping but joints and surfaces soon wore. Local carpenters and joiners made most machines, aided by the blacksmith. In addition to their normal hand tools the mechanical tools available were the treadle lathe for turning wood and, by 1760, the circular saw. Jesse Ramsden developed a screw cutting lathe in 1770, which cut fine threads suitable for micrometers but not ordinary screws. All tools had to be made by hand and many of the blades for edge tools were made by specialists in Sheffield. Other tools were made as a domestic industry. Men in Warrington, for

139

example, combined farming with file making until it became a factory industry about 1810.

Machine tools were developed by a number of inventors, often to solve problems encountered in making other new machines. Joseph Bramah, for example, designed a thief-proof lock in 1784. It would have cost far too much if he had made each part by hand for locks he wished to sell. Instead his assistant Henry Maudslay made a series of machines to cut parts for the locks. The machines making the sliders and keys were fitted with micrometers, so that no two locks were alike.

Maudslay set up his own firm in 1797, where he perfected the screw cutting lathe. He insisted that all machines should be made of metal, and required great accuracy from those who worked for him. Flat surfaces had to be tested against a standard surface kept in the workshop, and tool rests and micrometers measuring to 1/10,000 inch increased the accuracy. Maudslay made the set of block-making machines for the Admiralty to Marc Brunel's designs, 1802–7, which made it possible for ten men to produce 130,000 pulley blocks a year, in place of the hundred skilled craftsmen employed to make them before. This was a graphic example of what machine tools could do—there was a shortage of skilled men and their time could be used best if repetitive jobs could be left to machines.

Several of these early designers of machine tools worked in Manchester. Richard Roberts set up a workshop there in 1816; five years later he employed three men at 11s (55p) a week to drive machines (no steam engine here) and thirteen skilled craftsmen were paid 26–30s (£1.30–£1.50) a week. The firm produced lathes and planing machines for sale to other machine makers, and also textile machinery, locomotives, steam carriages and hole-punching machines. James Nasmyth was another engineer with works in Manchester. Apart from making most kinds of machine tools he invented several milling and shaping machines and, in 1839, a steam hammer. This was higher than a tilt hammer and could hit harder, and yet was under control—it could descend 'with power only sufficient to break an eggshell'. It was designed to forge the ever larger parts of locomotive and marine engines.

Page 141 (*above*) The prosperity of the cotton industry gave rise to very large mills, such as this near Stockport which was 300ft long. The separated chimney both gave greater height and removed the smoke. All processes were carried on in this mill, though many specialised in spinning only; (*below*) bleach fields were laid out in the eighteenth century, as here in Glasgow, for bleaching linen and cotton. The fields continued to be used after the introduction of bleaching powder for parts of dyeing processes.

Page 142 (*above*) The woollen industry moved into mills only slowly, and these were often sited in valleys to provide water. This mill was extended in the 1870s and since, though it is thought to be on the site of a manor mill. Weavers' cottages can be picked out by the long rows of windows on the upper floors; (*below*) an alum works early in the nineteenth century. Alum shale was quarried near Scarborough, burnt and placed in leaching pits. The resulting liquor was evaporated, allowing crystals to form.

ig 18 *Shaping the heads of screws* (left) *and cutting the threads by machinery* (right)

Joseph Whitworth, another tool maker working in Manchester, was one of the first to make a living just from machine tools. He also made his name by sorting the myriads of screw threads available in Britain before recommending a small number of standard sizes. Whitworth standards were accepted in Britain by the 1860s, making it much simpler to replace broken bolts and lost nuts. By that time the rest of Europe was using metric measurements.

The increasing use of machine tools had many consequences. The first was that the machines needed by the factory-based industries were stronger and more accurate, which made them better suited to working by steam power. Greater accuracy in making the parts led to smoother running. It also led to easier replacements. When a part broke on a hand-made machine the replacement had to be hand made, which was both expensive and involved long delays. Parts made with machine tools could be machined so accurately as to be identical and a replacement part could be ordered from stock.

I

This led to the idea of mass production, which was first practised in France in 1785 but is more usually associated with American industry. The shortage of skilled craftsmen there encouraged the more rapid adoption of machinery. Mass production was based on specialised machines, each of which carried out the same operation with great accuracy. All the parts were interchangeable and the finished product could be assembled from bins of parts. Since each part was made accurately, it was no longer necessary to file them before fitting them.

In the Crimea War (1854–6) blacksmiths went with troops to fashion new parts for damaged guns, because each gun was hand made and unique, and had to be repaired by hand. The Royal Small Arms Factory was set up at Enfield to make rifles by mass production methods, though few were made before the war ended. By 1857, the factory made 1,000 rifles a week, using 150 machine tools imported from the United States. Over 700 operations were needed from these machines to make each rifle. This kind of mass production could not have been achieved even by large numbers of craftsmen, for the parts could never have been made accurately enough to be interchangeable.

Mass production came to be used to manufacture a growing range of products, with America setting the pace. The production of sewing-machines, begun by Isaac Singer in 1851, is an example, and one that made cheaper clothes available through the shops. Mass production led to the production of a greater variety of goods and brought prices down.

Mass production was taken a stage further by Henry Ford in 1912 when he began his first assembly line in Detroit. His aim was to produce cars as economically as possible, and he decided that it would be cheaper to move the car to the many bins of parts than take handfuls of parts to assemble the car on one spot. The first production line was simple. A bare car chassis was pulled across the floor by a rope, and six assemblers added parts from bins at the side. The engine was lowered in with chains and the completed car taken away. So began flow production, with moving conveyors taking the growing product from one assembly point to the next. The method was soon copied by other car manufacturers, and has been adapted to other industries, such as

144

electric motors, where the numbers of products assembled justifies the high initial cost. Flow production was far in the future, however, when the railway engineers began their work.

TRANSPORT ENGINEERING

The development of the railways is outlined in chapter 18, and their importance in this chapter is as major consumers of iron and steel. Iron rails were increasingly used on the tramways in the eighteenth century, and all kinds of cross-sections were tried in an attempt to combine strength with cheapness. (The cost of wooden rails was estimated to be £440 per mile in 1797, and of iron rails in 1801 to be £1,500.) Cast iron was used until John Birkinshaw made several loads of wrought-iron rails at an ironworks in Bedlington in 1821. The cross-section of this was like an hour-glass and this shape became the standard rail on most British railways by the 1850s and remained so for a century. Bessemer steel was rolled into rails at Crewe in 1862, and these were used to replace iron rails as they were fifteen times more durable. Some Sheffield firms exported large tonnages of steel rails to America. Much of the steel output in the 1860s was used for rails, for the advantages of durability were greatest in products exposed to the weather.

Locomotive engineers worked on their own at first, enlisting the aid of local blacksmiths. George Stephenson's belief in the future of locomotives led him to form Robert Stephenson & Co in 1823 to build them at the celebrated Forth Street Works in Newcastle. Their small steam engine drove lathes, planers, drilling, punching and plate-shearing machines. Everything else was done by hand—wheels were driven on to axles with sledge hammers. *Locomotion* and *Rocket* were two of their products. The opening of the Liverpool and Manchester Railway in 1830 caused a great interest in railways. Richard Roberts in Manchester, Matthew Murray in Leeds, Neilson & Co in Glasgow and many others began designing and building locomotives for sale to railway companies and for export. The railway companies set up their own workshops and increasingly made all the rolling stock they needed. The Great Western Railway had the largest shops at Swindon, and other railways had workshops at Crewe,

Darlington and Glasgow. Many of the private builders changed to other forms of engineering, while some concentrated on the large export market for railway equipment. Not only were engines and rails exported but rolling stock, signalling equipment and even prefabricated bridges; 9,000 tons of parts for the Victoria Bridge, Montreal, were exported from Birkenhead between 1854 and 1859. The engineering companies, both railway and mixed, were in a good position to develop into a major industry, for they had the most modern machine tools, cheap iron from the new blast furnaces and unlimited power. As mentioned before, the railway companies quickly transferred to steel when it became available, and those connected with the industry continued to prosper to the end of the century. The world wars and intervening depression led to a loss of overseas markets. The railway workshops were firm believers in steam in the 1930s, and few firms seemed able to adapt their experience to the new fuels. The changeover to diesel-electric locomotives came suddenly in the 1960s, and with it the beginnings of electrification.

The manufacturers of railway equipment had had all the advantages, with new machinery and recently developed iron production methods with which to start a new industry. The shipbuilders were in a different position for they already had their own methods, developed for using wood. Completely new methods were needed to take advantage of iron and machinery. A further delaying factor was the seaman's suspicion of anything new, a natural reaction since his life was at stake should anything go wrong. The development of engineering among shipbuilders was therefore much slower than it had been with the railways, and there was a long overlapping period when both wooden and iron ships were built. The steam engine was the initial cause of the use of iron in ships, since the great weight of the engines made them a hazard in wooden hulls, as was the risk of fire.

Marine engines driving paddle wheels were fitted to a number of ships in America and Europe early in the nineteenth century. They were intended to supplement sails when the wind was not right. MatthewMurray made a high-pressure engine at the Leeds foundry which was fitted into a captured lugger, *L'Actif*, in 1811. The boat operated between Norwich and Yarmouth for many years. The firm made more marine engines for export, as did other engineers at the ports. As experience grew, larger engines were fitted into cross-channel packet boats, and as auxiliaries in trans-Atlantic sailing ships. The first trans-Atlantic steam ship, the *Great Western*, was still a wooden ship, though specially strengthened to take the stresses created by the engine.

Experience gained with that ship taught its designer, Isambard Brunel, that larger ships built of iron were needed to exploit marine engines to the full. His *Great Britain*, launched in 1843, was built entirely of iron and driven by a propeller instead of paddles. The commercial success of this ship encouraged other shipowners to build iron ships, and yards grew up in most large ports, especially from the mid-1860s.

The need for larger and specialised cargo ships in the 1880s coincided with the availability of cheap steel. The shipyards on the Tyne and Clyde led the industry from that time and continued to do so until 1920. British shipyards dominated world ship-building in that period. Of every thousand tons of shipping passing through the Suez Canal in 1896-7, 700 had been built in Britain, ninety-five in Germany and two in the United States. Britain was the largest exporter of ships—61 per cent of the world's merchant shipping was built in Britain, 1910-14. The American yards picked up some of this trade during the world war, but the British yards built two million tons in 1920. Then came the slump. Naval requirements dwindled because of disarmament, and British yards were not fitted to build the motor-driven ships that were now needed. The export trade dwindled and there was little demand for new ships in Britain—only 131,000 tons were launched in 1933, and 63 per cent of shipyard workers were unemployed. Building for British customers improved after that and was boosted by World War II but the export trade increasingly went to Germany and Japan.

The fortunes of the bicycle makers were rather better. The hobby horse of the eighteenth century gradually became the penny-farthing of the 1860s, made by many engineers in back street workshops. The industry settled in Coventry in 1869 and development began. Fifteen years later there were 200 varieties of bicycles, tricycles and others. In 1885, Rovers began manufacturing the safety bicycle with equal-sized wheels, and the pneumatic tyre invented by J. B. Dunlop the same year was a promise of comfort to come.

Petrol engines were imported in the 1890s and were adopted by the cycle manufacturers first, who made several kinds of power-assisted cycles. The widespread use of engines was discouraged, however, by the poor state of the roads and the repressive speed limits of the Red Flag Act. With the repeal of that Act in 1896 cycle manufacturers such as Humber, Rover and Singer turned to making cars and were joined by some general engineers. Each car was virtually hand built, since carbide cycle lamps and tyres were about the only parts that could be obtained from existing firms. As a result, cars were luxury items until 1914. Manufacturing methods lacked any real method at all; few manufacturers used any specialised machine tools of the kind used at Enfield. Two hundred makes of car were made in Britain before 1913 but no manufacturer could make more than one car a year for each man he employed. In America, by contrast, Ford employed 300 in 1904 and yet made 1,700 cars a year.

A vehicle industry began to emerge after 1918, based on machine tools and flow production techniques. Only ninety firms were still in business in 1920, and these were reduced to thirty-three by 1939 of which six made 90 per cent of the cars between them. Yet production of cars had increased from 32,000 in 1920 to 342,000 in 1939. Most car manufacturers were in the Birmingham–Coventry area, until William Morris set up works in Oxford, to be followed by others in the Home Counties, Cheshire, Lancashire and Linwood in Scotland. (Makers of components were scattered all over Britain by 1970.) British manufacturers had the advantage of new factories and machinery in the 1930s, which allowed them to increase their share of the export market at the expense of the German and American car producers. The export trade continued after World War II, especially in commercial vehicles, and helped to offset some of the losses in other branches of engineering. The home market grew rapidly, especially with the introduction of the baby car, starting with the Austin Seven, which sold for £165 in 1924.

The need for generating equipment, cables, switch-gear and consumer goods led to the growth of a new branch of engineering based on electricity. The first need had been for cables. It was known already that copper was a good conductor of electricity, and the problem was to find suitable insulating materials for mains cables. Ferranti developed the use of paper to separate concentric tubes of wire, and the whole cable was protected by steel wire. Rubber was used to cover domestic wiring by 1900. Electricity was principally used in the home for lighting at that time, and a number of firms made their own varieties of bulb, which even included cut glass ones. Tungsten was in general use as the filament by 1911, and the Westlake machine, making up to 100,000 bulbs a day, came into use in the 1930s. Ribbon machines were used twenty years later, making a million bulbs a day. Fluorescent lights were increasingly being used by then.

Electricity was expensive at the beginning of the twentieth century and there was no incentive to buy the fires and cookers that were being designed. The range and quality of these goods increased in the 1930s and became more attractive as electricity became available to more people. Firms established themselves, mostly in the South of England, and came into their own after the war in 1945. The use of electrical aids of all kinds spread rapidly in urban areas, though some of the more remote villages still had no electricity in 1970. Electrical engineering was by then an important element of the economy, supplying both private customers and other industries.

The aircraft industry developed from the 1920s to be another important branch of engineering, though relying more on aluminium than iron and steel. As with engineering generally, a large number of firms that began production were reduced to a handful by amalgamations and take-overs. In this way the industry was able to adapt itself to the increasing size and complexity of aircraft, both civil and military. Like so many of the recently formed industries, most firms were active in the South of England, where there was flatter land for runways and assembly hangers, several ports for importing raw materials and plenty of people seeking work.

A clear impression of the layout and working conditions in an eighteenth-century tool works can be gained from a visit to the Finch Brothers Foundry, Sticklepath, Devon, or the Abbeydale Industrial Hamlet, Sheffield. Various machine tools and a gunsmith's workshop can be seen in the Birmingham Museum of Science and Industry, and other aspects of the iron and steel industries are shown in the Industrial Museum of South Wales, Swansea, and the Museum of Science and Engineering, Newcastle upon Tyne. Shipbuilding is featured in the Maritime Museum, Hartlepool, Co Durham, and electronics in the Independent Broadcasting Authority's Television Gallery in London.

15 King Cotton or Rayon Republic?

Taken together, the textile industries experienced all the effects of industrial revolution. There were many inventions, each helping to remove one bottleneck after another in the involved processes concerned. These inventions were promptly and widely used, particularly in the cotton industry. That industry was also alive to the advantages to be gained by using steam power and large mills, and Sir Richard Arkwright, one of the most famous of cotton spinners, originated methods of factory organisation and business management to match the new mills.

Massive investment in mills and machinery (Arkwright had invested £200,000 by 1782) led to rapid increases in production, which continued until 1920. Other results also attracted notice, particularly the working conditions within mills. The long hours, pittance wages, dangerous and unhealthy working conditions and in particular the treatment of children in the mills were subjects of denunciation from 1800 onwards. Some of the critics were landowners like Lord Shaftesbury. He was genuinely appalled at conditions in factories and mines, and spent a lifetime in parliament pressing for laws to bring about improvements. The factory owners (and their representatives in parliament—in particular those MPs who sat for constituencies in the northern industrial areas) pointed out that the farm labourers on Shaftesbury's own estates in Dorset lived and worked in even worse conditions than the factory labourers—but nobody was championing their cause.

Other critics were men like William Cobbett, the radical journalist, who wrote about political matters and about contemporary rural life. Cobbett believed that the acceleration of industry had done nothing but harm, and that the British people had been better off when they made a living from the land and lived close to nature; he thought that industrialisation had corrupted both life and politics. He thundered away at manufacturers in his weekly newspaper, the *Political Register*. In 1824, for example, he wrote that:

Some of these lords of the loom have in their employ thousands of miserable creatures. In the cotton-spinning work these creatures are kept, fourteen hours in each day, locked up, summer and winter, in a heat of from EIGHTY TO EIGHTY-FOUR DEGREES . . .

Now, then, do you duly consider what a heat of eight-four is? Very seldom do we feel such a heat as this in England. The 31st of last August, and the 1st, 2nd and 3rd of last September, were very hot days. The newspapers told us that men had dropped down dead in the harvest fields and that many horses had fallen dead upon the road; and yet the heat during those days never exceeded eighty-four degrees in the hottest part of the day. We were retreating to the coolest rooms in our houses; we were pulling off our coats, wiping the sweat off our faces, puffing, blowing and panting; and yet we were living in a heat nothing like eighty degrees. What, then, must be the situation of the poor creatures who are doomed to toil, day after day, for three hundred and thirteen days in the year, fourteen hours in each day, in an average heat of eighty-two degrees? Can any man, with a heart in his body, and a tongue in his head, refrain from cursing a system that produces such slavery and such cruelty?

Although Cobbett, in his anger, forgot the long hours that people spent farming, in all weathers (or, at least, felt that that hardship was better than factory work), there was much in factory conditions that called for urgent reform. Factory Acts were passed from 1802, mainly to limit hours, and the 1833 Act appointed factory inspectors to make spot checks on mills. Conditions seemed worse in the cotton industry than the other textile trades largely because it adopted mill methods first. These were entirely new to Britain on the scale used by the cotton manufacturers and were bound to cause comment. Conditions in the other textile industries were often no better but attracted less comment because the pace of change was far slower and many processes were still being done domestically. Working conditions in some industries were far worse than the cotton mills but went unreformed because people were accustomed to them being like that, or chose to ignore them. The rapid growth of the cotton industry, the high mills and large numbers employed, and the sudden wealth of the manufacturers singled them out for comment, some of which was inspired by political as much as humanitarian instincts.

Innovation in the textile industries was uneven. The first cotton mills were built in the 1770s, and many were in production by 1800. The first worsted mills were being built by then, and that industry was substantially mill-based by 1830. The woollen industry, once the giant among textiles, was slower to adopt the new methods. This was in part due to its past importance; manufacturers were content to continue with the old methods, and the laws that had helped them in times past now hindered development. There were also difficulties in adapting the new machines to handle the softer woollen yarn and there was no need for large mills until there were alternatives to domestic machinery. While some processes could be better done in mills in the 1790s, the use of the power loom for woollen cloth production did not become general until the 1860s, and the purpose-built woollen mills date from then.

The linen and silk industries also expanded in the nineteenth century as demand increased. A number of machines, many of them designed by Matthew Murray, made the processing of flax cheaper, and the manufacture of linen in mills developed slowly in Yorkshire, Scotland and, later, Ireland. The industry could never compete with cotton for cheapness and variety, though the production of canvas was in constant demand for sailing ships. Peak production was reached in the linen industry in the 1870s, after which a long slow decline set in. The silk industry followed a similar pattern, its decline being brought about by the introduction of much cheaper artificial silk (rayon).

The cotton and wool industries lost many of their export markets during World War I which was the more serious for those employed in cotton who depended on exports. The industries also experienced increasing competition from the man-made fibres, especially after 1945. Cloth production from these synthetic materials became a separate branch of the textile trade and caused problems to the traditional fibre users. With this pattern in mind it will be easier to consider fibres individually.

The production of cotton cloth was still banned in 1750. The prohibition, imposed in 1721, had been eased a little in 1736 to allow the manufacture of fustians, which were mixtures of wool/cotton and linen/cotton. Further concessions were made in 1774 but that many people ignored the law may be guessed from the fact that the output of cotton cloth surpassed that of wool early in the nineteenth century. Its manufacture was carried on in many areas in 1750 but mainly around the ports of London, Bristol, Liverpool and Glasgow. The industry was totally dependent on imported raw materials, and was limited by the small amounts of expensive cotton available from India and the Middle East. The invention of the cotton gin in 1793 made possible limitless quantities of much cheaper American cotton, and the later development of the industry was based on this. Imports leapt from 11·8 million lb in 1782 to 56 million lb in 1802.

Most of the necessary machines had been developed by that time to overcome the existing slow machines. Cotton manufacturing had taken root in areas where woollen cloth was made, and used woollen tools and looms. The fineness of cotton thread made production very slow since it was impossible to speed up hand processes. There was an immense market for cotton cloth if only it could be made, for people could afford more cotton clothing than wool, and could wash it more easily. Cotton merchants had everything to gain from finding faster manufacturing methods.

The immediate bottleneck was in spinning, since ten women with Saxony wheels were needed to keep one handloom weaver going, or forty if the loom had been fitted with the flying shuttle invented by John Kay in 1733. James Hargreaves invented a spinning jenny in 1765, which could spin sixteen threads at a time. It was a hand-driven machine designed for children to work at home, and the yarn was suitable for weft though not strong enough for warp. Richard Arkwright took the credit for inventing the water frame in 1769, though the basic idea had been devised by Thomas Highs. Though first driven by a horse gin, the frame really needed water power to spin a strong yarn suitable for warps, and it was installed in new river-side mills. Ideas from both machines were incorporated in the design of the spinning mule by Samuel Crompton in 1779. This small machine was used in cottages at first, and worked by hand. The dual-purpose yarn was so good, however, that mules were soon extended to more than a hundred spindles and had to be installed in mills. These machines resulted in plentiful supplies of yarn by 1780. Arkwright had improved existing carding machines by this time so that he had a continuous power driven process from cleaned raw cotton to spun yarn. The invention of a new machine did not mean that older ones were instantly scrapped; there was much overlapping. Manchester fustian makers in 1790 were supplied with warps by merchants, which were probably mule spun, but spun their own weft on jennies.

Arkwright's first mill was at Cromford in Derbyshire, and cotton spinning developed in that area, supplying yarn to the East Midlands hosiery knitters as well as for cotton cloth. Cotton mills spread to Cheshire and sprang up in Lancashire—twenty-five mills were built in Stockport, in 1770–90, and as many in Oldham, in 1776–88. Many of these were water powered but, from the installation of a Boulton and Watt engine in a mill in Papplewick, Nottinghamshire in 1785 the use of engines in mills became common and led to the rapid growth of the industry in the nineteenth century. Mills also sprang up on the Clyde, of which the most famous were those at New Lanark managed by Robert Owen, who showed that a mill could be profitable and yet offer shorter hours and higher wages than most. Cotton spinning took root in other areas, such as Bristol and Rochdale–Huddersfield but tended to ebb and flow with the varying fortunes of the cotton and wool trades.

The combination of new machinery, an increased labour force and mill methods reduced the cost of making yarn by 90 per cent between 1770 and 1812. Adapting power to weaving took longer so that, while 90,000 mill workers were employed in 1806 to carry out all processes except weaving, 184,000 handloom weavers were needed to keep pace. Most of these worked in their own homes on looms installed by their employers. This gave them little independence, for the industry was controlled by a relatively small number of manufacturers like Arkwright, Jedediah Strutt and Samuel Oldknow, who regulated the amount of yarn available and put it out for weaving. A power loom had been invented by Edmund Cartwright in 1787 but many improvements were needed before it came into general use in the 1820s. By that time cloth was being printed much faster with cylinders instead of wooden blocks positioned by hand, and the new chemical bleach powder had made bleaching a matter of hours instead of months. The imports of raw cotton indicate the spectacular growth in the industry, before its decline after 1920:

Average annual imports in million lbs			
1820s	173	1880s	1,473
1830s	348	1890s	1,556
1840s	550	1900s	1,733
1850s	795	1910s	1,875
1860s	801	1920s	1,488
1870s	1,244	1930s	1,360

Most of this growth was brought about using the machinery mentioned, but continuous improvements were made. Mules of more than 400 spindles were being made by 1800, and Richard Roberts made the machine automatic in 1825 so that it could continue spinning yarn as long as there was slubbing to draw out. Roberts also made improved power looms, using cast-iron frames. Ring spinning frames were introduced from America about 1850 but mules remained the more popular. Improved steam engines allowed larger mills and some family businesses grew very large. Apart from the period 1861–5, when civil war in America cut off supplies and left firms dependent on the Middle East, cotton manufacturers saw few problems.

Increasingly in the nineteenth century, cotton goods were exported, particularly to America and Asia. The value of cotton goods exported in 1881 was £80 million, about a third of the value of all exports (£234 million). Again, of eight milliard yards (8,000 million) of cotton cloth produced in 1913, seven milliard were exported. The amount of textile machinery exported between these dates steadily increased, and a time was bound to come when the importing countries would be less dependent on Lancashire, then producing the bulk of the cloth. World War I determined the time, for the lack of ships to carry goods encouraged Japan, India and other countries to develop their own cotton mills. The depression reduced still further the demand for sheetings and shirtings, and output fell drastically—4·5 milliard yards were produced in 1937, of which only 2 milliard were exported. Unemployment, short-time working and bankruptcies were serious, with Lancashire the hardest hit. Employment fell by 43 per cent, 1921–38. Some firms tried blending cotton with the new rayon but customers were suspicious. The tyre producers were better customers, needing increasing quantities of yarn to keep pace with the car manufacturers. Despite improved trading in World War II, it was clear by 1950 that the prosperous days would never return. Mill closures, mergers, take-overs and legislation (1959) combined to reduce the number of firms left in the industry, and they increasingly explored the possibilities of synthetic fibres.

LINEN AND SILK

The linen and cotton industries were about equal in 1750. Flax grew in many parts of Britain, and was manufactured nearby, particularly in the Lake District, West Yorkshire, Lancashire, the East Midlands and South West. The home crop was supplemented with yarn from Scotland and north-west Europe, and flax from Ireland and the Baltic. The Irish linen industry was rigidly controlled in the interests of English manufacturers, but efforts to expand the Scottish industry met with some success at the end of the eighteenth century. By that time machines for hackling the flax were being developed, though spinning machines and looms were not successfully adapted to handle flax until the mid-nineteenth century.

A number of large firms (such as Marshalls in Leeds) dominated the industry for much of the nineteenth century. These firms surpassed the domestic industry in other towns, such as Barnsley and Knaresborough. However, the English linen firms found costs too high when flax ceased to be grown in any quantity, and many went out of business after 1870. This left the market to the many smaller firms in Ireland and Angus, Fife and Perth. These firms represented a protracted development dating from about 1750 in Scotland and 1810 in Ireland, which had been brought about by government encouragement, the laying down of bleach fields and, later, the manufacture of bleaching chemicals, and the continuing demand for fine linen for the table and bed, as well as clothing. Supplying a steady market, these firms were able to withstand twentieth-century upheavals far more easily than the cotton firms.

The silk industry was necessarily small, handling an expensive raw material that, in the eighteenth century, could only be used for luxury goods. The raw silk was imported, largely from Italy, and was thrown—a number of filaments were drawn out and lightly twisted to be strong enough to be woven on handlooms.

Early in the nineteenth century, spinning mills began to treat waste silk in the same way as cotton to produce cheaper silk goods such as scarves and handkerchiefs. This trade was largely centred in Manchester, while similar mills in Yorkshire supplied the worsted industry with yarn for fancy cloths. The whole industry prospered throughout the nineteenth century but artificial silk and other synthetic fibres left silk as very much a luxury material and the industry declined a little before stabilising to supply goods solely for the luxury market.

WORSTED

The worsted industry was quite evenly divided between East Anglia and Yorkshire by 1750 but, while the East Anglian manufacturers kept to traditional methods, the Yorkshiremen were seeking ways to expand production of a cloth in great demand. There was talk of industrial espionage—employees of a Halifax firm were sent to Norwich to learn better ways of making crêpe and bombazine cloths. More was to be gained by adapting the new spinning machinery to spin worsted yarn. The industry was dominated by men who were both manufacturers and mer-

Page 159 (*above*) Tallow, soda and other ingredients were boiled in large coppers. The liquid soap was taken from these and poured into wooden frames to solidify. The soap was cut into blocks with 'cheese' wire; (*below*) the manufacture of footwear grew from a local craft into a factory industry in the nineteenth century. This reconstructed clogger's shop is an example of the village manufacturer. The patterns for the uppers hang on the wall, and below them is the bench for cutting soles.

Page 160 (*above*) This drawing aptly illustrates the transformation brought about by railways. The heavy carrier's wagon can manage not more than walking pace with perhaps a ton of goods, while the locomotive draws a long train at some speed; (*below*) few people saw this petrol wagon as a threat to the railways when Leylands made it in 1911. The greater flexibility of lorries over railways proved to be very popular.

chants, because the raw materials were expensive and few cottagers could have handled the trade themselves. The manufacturers employed people to spin and weave the cloth in their homes, supplying them with combed wool. This involved much fetching and carrying, which added to costs. The water frame was adapted to spin worsted yarn about 1780, when it became known as the throstle, and required water power to work it. The manufacturers therefore began building mills, and the area around Bradford and Halifax became the centre of the industry. Steam power supplemented water, and the local coal gave the Yorkshire industry a clear advantage over East Anglia.

The slowest part of the worsted process was the preparation of the tops from which the yarn was spun. These had to be combed from raw wool, a skilled task done with hand combs heated over a charcoal stove. Edmund Cartwright invented a combing frame in 1789 which could do the work of twenty combers. This aroused opposition from the hand-combers, despite their fume-laden workshops, and the machine caught on slowly, until it was improved in 1827. It made worsted production a factory industry, even though the weaving was done on handlooms until the 1830s. These were often set up in the mills, to safeguard quality and keep patterns secret, but some weaving was put out to domestic workers. The power loom came into use in the 1830s —2,768 were in use in 1836, 11,458 in 1841 and 16,870 in 1843. Virtually all of these were in Yorkshire as the East Anglian producers could not compete and steadily went out of business. The handloom weavers in Yorkshire were faced with falling wages and abject poverty but clung to their trade as long as they could. There was little work for them in the mills for the power looms were supervised by women.

The industry continued to expand, though facing increasing competition from French manufacturers towards the end of the century. A number of major technical improvements were made to the combing machines by Donisthorpe and Lister in 1851 and Noble in 1887. The American ring-spinning frame began to replace the throstle in the 1880s, and the automatic Northrop loom began to be used after 1900. World War I and the depression that followed caused difficulties, as in all the established industries. Exports dwindled during the war and did not wholly revive afterwards. The damage was not as serious as in the cotton industry for a higher proportion of goods had always been sold in Britain.

The industry began to modernise itself in the 1950s. Steam power was replaced by electricity, and blends of wool and synthetic fibres developed to produce permanent creases, easier washing and similar advantages. Much of the old machinery began to be replaced with new, which increasingly came from Germany and Switzerland which had taken the lead in making fast machines. As in the cotton industry, mergers, closures and takeovers resulted in the industry being controlled by a small number of very large combines.

WOOL

The woollen industry was still a national industry in 1750 with production taking place everywhere. Much of this was to satisfy village needs, while the South West and Yorkshire were the leading areas producing surpluses for export. The machines invented for the cotton industry were of no immediate use and, quite apart from that, the industry was not organised in a way that could take advantage of the new developments.

More cloth was needed in the eighteenth century. Cotton was preferable to cheap woollens for petticoats and scarves but the rapidly expanding population still needed more woollen cloth than ever. The raw wool came partly from native sheep, and included the noils (the short fibres) rejected by the worsted combers, but increasing quantities of wool from Ireland in the 1760s, and then Spain, Portugal, Germany and (from 1818) Australia were imported for the better cloths.

The industry continued to be dominated in the South West by a small number of merchant-manufacturers. They bought the raw material, put it out for working into cloth, and controlled the finishing processes and merchanting. These were wealthy enough to have built mills and installed machines but a lack of enterprise and a shortage of power led to missed opportunities. Instead, the industry expanded mostly in the Huddersfield–Wakefield area of Yorkshire, and in Ayrshire and around Galashiels. While these were the centres, many individuals carried on a thriving trade in quite other areas, and the industry did not contract into one area.

The adaptation of machinery proceeded slowly. It began with the carding engine. The one developed by Arkwright could be used with only minor changes for wool, but it needed power to work it. Unlike the cotton and woollen industries, mills already existed in the woollen industry for fulling cloth. Enterprising owners installed a carding machine in the mill and drove it with spare power available between fulling. In doing so, one of the children's jobs moved from the home to a mill, and the transfer of the industry had begun. Scribbling machines were added to the mills about 1800, and the scribblings were taken back to the cottage to be spun on a jenny. (Scribblings were a halfway stage between loose fibres and spun yarn; a better yarn was spun from scribblings than could be spun straight from carded wool.) Some of the workers were having work put out to them by merchants, some of whom also supplied the machines, but it was more common in Yorkshire for the clothier to own his tools and buy either raw or scribbled wool.

The industry expanded rapidly from about 1800, with a great need for cloth both for the growing population and the many armies allied against France. Benjamin Gott was one of the biggest army contractors as well as supplying cloth for general sale. He planned a mill in Leeds in 1792 for all processes from sorting the wool to packing pieces; by 1830 he employed 1,300 people in three mills but all the weavers still used handlooms, and their output was supplemented by independent clothiers. He was almost unique, for the normal pattern in 1830 was for the handloom weavers to fetch spun yarn from the mills, which were beginning to use mules for spinning. By this stage all the processes had become mill-based except weaving and the weakness of woollen weft meant that power looms had to be run so slowly that they were uneconomic. So, when the women and children went to work in the mills, the men stayed at home to weave. Large numbers of homes were built which might be called cottage factories. These were frequently three-storey cottages, with the home in the lower two floors and the looms housed on the top

163

floor. This was a separate lock-up workshop, in which the weaver and perhaps his sons or wage-earning weavers worked all the daylight hours. The pieces of cloth were taken to the mill for fulling, dried on tenter frames and sold in the cloth halls, such as may still be seen in Halifax and Penistone. Changes in fashion from plain colour cloths to tweeds led to weavers making goods to order for merchants, and trade in the halls declined. Improvements in power looms, exhibited in 1851, made them more suitable for weaving woollens and larger mills were built from the 1860s onwards to house all the processes, whether for making cloths to wear, blankets or carpets. The handloom weavers kept working in declining numbers until about 1900, although some stayed in business longer, especially in the Hebrides.

Although the industry depended to a great extent on imported wool, mere figures of imports do not give an accurate impression of the growth of the industry. Quite an amount of British wool was also used, and there are few reliable figures about that. In addition, the industry increasingly used reclaimed wool which the shoddy and mungo trade prepared from cast-off clothes. About 40 per cent of the wool used to make cloth in 1880 had been reclaimed in this way. As a result, cloth was cheaper and it was possible to have swiftly changing fashions in the colour, design and style of clothes.

Although exports of cloth were important, sales to the home market accounted for much of the industry's output, which made it less vulnerable to the depression. Trading was difficult but not hopeless. As with worsted firms, woollen manufacturers began to modernise after 1950. Water wheels and steam engines made way for electric motors, though turbines were sometimes used to make firms self-supporting in electricity. Foreign looms were imported (though good cloth design was more valuable than fast production), and synthetic fibres used to make blends. The industry remained mainly dispersed into many medium-sized firms for it had to be quick to adapt to changing fashions. The one main technical change was to make jersey knitted fabrics when they became fashionable in the late 1960s. The industry contracted, like the cotton and worsted industries, as the synthetic manufacturers took an increasing share of production. Many of the firms in the South West and Scotland closed, and the industry entrenched itself in Yorkshire.

The discovery and development of man-made fibres is an interesting story, which can only be touched on briefly in a book of this length. It began in 1892, when Cross and Bevan made rayon (artificial silk) from wood pulp. This was used in about 1912 to make stockings in place of cotton and worsted but only served to boost the production of silk stockings. Courtaulds used a cotton/rayon blend for shirts from 1919 but men's fashions were slow to change and the demand for those and for suits of wool/rayon was only just beginning to grow in 1939. However, much had been learned about how to dye the new fibre and the public had learned what to expect.

Nylon was discovered by the American Wallace Carothers. Nylon stockings arrived in Britain in 1939 and sixty-four million pairs sold in the first twelve months. Courtaulds and ICI together formed British Nylon Spinners in 1940, and used the yarns for parachutes, glider ropes and cord. After the war they opened a vast factory at Pontypool in 1948 and others in Doncaster and Gloucester, and set about supplying yarns suitable for every purpose from delicate underwear to tarpaulins and safety belts.

The process of making nylon began with polymer chips from the chemical works. These were heated and extruded through spinnerets, like water from a watering can, though much finer. The filaments were cooled, which hardened them, so that they could be stretched which made them strong, white and shiny. They could then be used in two ways. Yarns for fabrics such as stockings were made by lightly twisting filaments together, as with silk. The denier scale was worked out to measure these. Alternatively, the filaments were chopped into short lengths and crimped. Called stable fibre, this could be spun and woven on conventional textile machinery, or blended with wool or cotton first.

Already nylon had been joined by terylene, discovered by J. R. Whinfield in 1941 and developed by ICI after the war in a new factory at Wilton, Yorkshire. This had some advantages over nylon, such as being resistant to creasing and shrinking, and was blended with wool by the worsted industry to make suit cloths for those reasons. The established textile industries made use of the new materials in blends or exclusively—some former cotton mills changed completely. In addition some new mills appeared, mainly in the Midlands, producing crimplene materials.

There were many kinds of man-made fibre in use by 1970, many of them being trade names for nylon and terylene. Glass fibre was one of the more interesting of the others, and was used for soft furnishings. The use of paper to make clothes was also being explored, and the use of non-woven materials of synthetic fibres bonded with adhesives was tried. There were advantages in hygiene in being able to use throw-away tea towels and clothes but the fabrics were still too expensive for people to prefer cleanliness. Paper and non-woven clothing proved more popular in the United States.

The choice of fabrics had increased dramatically since 1750. Most of the population then had one suit of clothes which they wore until it wore out. Cleanliness was difficult since woollen clothing was hard both to wash and to dry. The cotton industry provided a cheap alternative for many woollen clothes and greatly improved the range of clothes most people could afford. Technical changes in the textile and other industries made rapid expansion possible and reduced production costs for all the traditional fibres. While these were affected by the range of fibres available from the chemical industry, the whole textile industry was in a position to provide a wide range of goods at all prices by 1970, whether for clothing or household and industrial purposes.

PLACES TO VISIT

The developments in cotton machinery can best be seen by visiting the Old House Museum, Bakewell, Derbyshire, and in Lancashire the Lewis Museum of Textile Machinery, Blackburn, the Tonge Moor Texile Machinery Museum, Bolton and Helmshore Museum. Bradford Industrial Museum has concentrated on worsted machinery, which is kept in working order. The development of the woollen industry nationally is shown in no museum, and the interested visitor has a long journey ahead of him. An entire woollen mill has been moved to the Welsh Folk Museum at St Fagan's, Cardiff, and is worked. A handloom weaver's cottage is on show at Kilbarchan, Renfrew, and a cottage factory of 1840 has been restored as the Colne Valley Museum, Golcar, Huddersfield. Surely there is scope for a national wool textile museum in one of the wool manufacturing regions? A display of lace making has been set up at the Nottingham Industrial Museum, and linen and silk looms can be seen in the Bridewell Museum, Norwich.

16 Acids, Alkalis and Alkathene

The expansion of industry was greatly aided by the development of the chemical industries, and became dependent on them for synthetic materials as supplies of the natural raw materials dwindled. Supplies of sour milk and sunlight, for example, which the textile industries had always used for bleaching their cloths, could not possibly have been increased in step with the increasing demand for fabrics. Glass production was dependent on increasing supplies of soda. In the twentieth century, the high price of timber and metals put the new electrical goods out of the reach of most people until alternatives were developed from plastics. This was a far cry from seventeenth-century salt pans.

CHEMICALS

The development of chemical production stemmed from the need for heavy chemicals such as sulphuric acid, or vitriol as it was known in the eighteenth century. It was used by tin-platers, refiners, bleachers and the makers of mordants, which were used by dyers to make a cloth 'take' a dye. Commercial production began in Twickenham in 1736, where Joshua Ward used a bank of fifty-gallon glass flasks laid on their sides. Sulphur and nitre, burnt in the necks of the flasks, produced gases which were absorbed by water in the flasks. The weak acid was later distilled to increase its strength. While this was a great improvement and brought down the cost of the acid, the process was too slow to meet the needs of industry. Ten years later in Birmingham, John Roebuck burnt the same mixture over water inside lead chambers. He moved to Scotland and set up a works at Prestonpans in 1749; the increased efficiency of the process reduced costs by three-quarters. This brought the price within the reach of bleachers, and greatly increased the demand for the acid, though many firms still relied on sunlight to judge from the many bleach-fields opened in Scotland after 1750. Roebuck did not patent the lead chamber process, and firms using it began in London (1772), Bury (1783), Bradford (1792)—a total of twenty-three by 1820. By that time bleachmakers were setting up their own acid works, starting with Charles Tennant at St Rollox (Glasgow) in 1803. The use of steam in place of water and blowing the gases into the chamber made the process continuous in the 1830s, and further modifications made it highly efficient by 1870s. Experiments were already taking place to perfect the cheaper contact process at that time but there was no incentive for firms to change to this process until more acid was needed to make explosives during World War I. Government factories were set up then, and a large plant was built at Billingham in 1930 near the anhydrite mines which supplied the raw material. Others followed at Widnes and Whitehaven in the 1950s, and 90 per cent of sulphuric acid was made by the contact process in 1970.

Nicholas Leblanc invented a process for making soda in 1791, which used sulphuric acid and salt. Soda was in continuous demand for the manufacture of soap and glass. The Losh brothers began using the process at Newcastle in the 1790s, and James Muspratt at Liverpool in 1823. Leblanc's process allowed large amounts of hydrochloric acid gas to be released into the air, which blighted the landscape around any alkali works. Muspratt was forced to close his Liverpool works because of the pollution it caused, and opened others in St Helens, Flint and Widnes. A number of firms set up works on Tyneside, of which Allhusens was the largest.

The main outlet for firms using the Leblanc process was the need for soda to make the hard soap used in washing textiles. Animal fat or vegetable oils, caustic soda and water were boiled in pans or kettles (plate 143). The addition of salt caused soap to form as a curd, which was scooped off and pressed. The waste, called soapers salts, was sold back to the alkali manufacturers as a source of salt, until Alfred Nobel discovered that the glycerine in soapers salts could be made into dynamite. He set up a works to produce nitroglycerine at Ardeer, Ayrshire, in 1871, and used soapers salts as a supply of glycerine. Soda was also needed by the makers of toilet soap. Andrew Pears had started making transparent soap at his London works in 1789 but it was made a household name by advertisements using the painting *Bubbles* in the 1870s and on the backs of postage stamps in 1881. The soap industry was developing rapidly in Lancashire at that time, and was coming to be dominated by William Lever, who opened a vast new works at Port Sunlight in 1888. He steadily bought up rival manufacturers and suppliers of raw materials. Since these were mostly vegetable oils, it seemed logical to combine with Jurgens, makers of margarine, to form Unilever in 1929.

The pollution caused by the Leblanc process was solved in 1836 with the development of the Gossage tower, which converted gas into hydrochloric acid. The bleaching power of chlorine had been shown by another Frenchman, Claude Berthollet, in 1785. This had been put into use in Glasgow by James Watt in 1787, and was soon copied by cotton firms in Aberdeen and Manchester. Charles Macintosh, who worked for Tennants, invented a dry bleaching powder in 1799, and the firm began production immediately. The effect was startling—the cost of bleaching a twenty-five yard piece of cotton fell from 7s (35p) to 6d (2½p) in 1800 alone, and the price of bleaching powder made at St Rollox fell from £140 per ton then to £60 in 1820. The demand for chlorine continued to grow, and the use of Gossage towers was made compulsory in the Alkali Act, 1863. The hydrochloric acid that had once been waste was now the profitable product of the alkali firms, which increasingly sold soda at a loss.

Work in these firms was specialised by the end of the nineteenth century, and also dangerous. Men raking the saltcake were exposed to rushes of hydrochloric acid gas which rotted their teeth. Works in Jarrow began to mechanise some processes in 1853 but it was a long time before this became general. On the other hand firms came to employ analytical chemists, both to maintain the quality of products and to develop new ones from other wastes. The major firms combined in 1890 to form United Alkali Ltd in the face of a declining demand for their products.

This was due to the more direct Solvay process which had been slowly perfected by Ludwig Mond and John Brunner. The development was long and difficult, and led to a number of Brunner-Mond subsidiaries, such as Synthetic Ammonia and Nitrates Ltd at Billingham-on-Tees and the Mond Nickel Co at Clydach, Swansea. The Solvay process was commercially viable by 1930 and the Leblanc firms were rendered uneconomic.

Another new branch of the chemicals industry (based on coal) grew up in the nineteenth century. Some of the varied uses of coal had been known for some time; coal gas had been effectively used by William Murdock in 1792, while Abraham Darby had used coke in 1709. Some people tried to obtain other products. Johann Becher took out an English patent in 1681 for the preparation of tar from coal but died the next year. Just a century later, Lord Dundonald set up tar kilns at Culross, Fife. Tar was needed by the Admiralty, for caulking wooden hulls and decks, and Charles Macintosh showed the properties of paper coated with tar on the roof of his alum works. Dundonald established the British Tar Company in 1786, and built kilns at Muirkirk, Ayrshire, and in Coalbrookdale but his ventures were not successful. Other inventors added their thoughts in the nineteenth century and the by-products of gas works and the needs of industry finally launched the coal tar industry. The range of products obtainable from coal, and the number of firms involved, steadily increased. In Bristol, for example, the firm of Butlers separated coal tar into pitch and oils. They burnt the pitch to make lamp black, and the oils included creosote (used by Brunel to preserve railway sleepers), benzole and naphthalene. Macintosh had found that tar spirit dissolved rubber, as will be seen later. Further refining produced raw materials for artificial fertilisers, high explosives, pharmaceutical products and, by the 1930s, plastics.

The discovery by William Perkin in 1856 that a mauve dye could be extracted from naphthalene marked the start of a separate line of research. He discovered a red dye in 1869 and he and other researchers in Lancashire added many more by 1900. Up to this time, natural dyes had been made from lichens, logwood, plants and shells. It had proved steadily more difficult to find sufficient quantities as the amount of cloth produced increased. The discovery and development of artificial dyes could not have come at a better time, and the quantities used in textile finishing steadily increased. However, 90 per cent of the dyes used were imported from Germany, and not only did the inventors show no interest in making them in Britain but neither did anyone else. A number of dyestuffs makers grouped themselves around the Huddersfield firm of Read, Holliday & Sons after 1900, and ultimately became the British Dyestuffs Corporation, adding Scottish Dyes Ltd in 1925. This group produced an increasing proportion of the dyes used in Britain. Imports of dyes had risen steadily to reach £14 million in 1920, and then abruptly fell as the British firms went into full production.

The firms involved had learnt during World War I that an industrial country could not afford either to neglect research or to allow its inventions to be developed abroad. The naval blockade left many textile firms stranded for lack of their accustomed dyes and other materials. Research and development are both expensive, and the larger chemical firms came to the conclusion that they should pool their resources to provide for research and to eliminate waste. Accordingly the United Alkali Co, British Dyestuffs Corporation, Brunner, Mond and Co Ltd and Nobel Industries combined in 1926 to form Imperial Chemical Industries, with total assets of £56 million. While many smaller chemical firms continued in their own fields, ICI increasingly dominated every aspect of chemicals production, and examples of this will be seen later in the chapter.

RUBBER AND PLASTICS

The small quantity of rubber that was used before 1820 was made into poor quality tubing, used by doctors and in laboratories. Then Thomas Hancock found a better way of preparing the rubber for use, making it possible to make sheets of any size and also thread. Hancock and his brother were experimenting with open-sided steam carriages, and therefore had an interest in waterproof clothing for their passengers. Shortly afterwards, Charles Macintosh found that oils derived from coal tar served as rubber solvents, thus laying the way for spreading rubber on cloth, which was the first kind of 'macintosh'. The two men formed a partnership, based on the factory Macintosh had opened in Manchester in 1824, and made waterproofed clothing and shoe soles. Rubber was also increasingly used in surgery and engineering—imports rose from twenty-three tons in 1830 to 330 tons in 1840.

A year later, Charles Goodyear invented the process of vulcanisation, which made rubber harder by heating it and adding sulphur. Harder rubber was more suitable for shoe soles, and was also used to make hoses and conveyor belts, while thin sheets of it made a lighter macintosh. The development of cheap transport encouraged the use of waterproof clothing, and also used rubber in other ways. The railways incorporated rubber in buffers and springs, while Hancock made solid rubber tyres for cycles. John Dunlop invented the all-rubber pneumatic tyre in 1888, which was quickly taken up by the cycle makers. Michelin made them for cars in 1895 and Dunlops followed in 1900. Imports reached 20,000 tons in that year, and the electrical industry was using a great part of that as insulation. The supply of rubber had been made more certain by a rare piece of foresight—2,000 young plants were sent from Kew Gardens in London to Ceylon in 1877. These were soon distributed in Malaya and other Asian countries, and began to add to rubber supplies in 1895. The consumption of rubber continued to grow after 1900, the motor and aircraft industries being major consumers. Supplies were difficult to obtain in World War II, which encouraged the use of synthetic rubber, which had been developed in 1926 in Russia. This was but one of many plastics which came to be used in place of rubber wherever there was an alternative, though it was not the first to have been invented.

'Plastics' is a group name for a large number of substances, just as 'textiles' includes cotton, wool, silk and others. Though the plastics industry is recent, plastics began in 1862 with the discovery of a substance by Alexander Parkes which he called parkesine. He was no businessman and did nothing with his discovery. In the United States, however, John Hyatt renamed it celluloid, patented it in 1869, and began production with the Albany Dental Plate Company. Production was finally started in

Britain by the British Xylonite Company in 1877. Celluloid was never produced in quantity because it was difficult to work and highly inflammable. It found uses in time for such articles as spectacle frames, fountain pen barrels and table tennis balls, while the birth of the cinema provided a new market for large quantities.

A more versatile form of plastic was invented by Leo Baekeland in America in 1907, and was called bakelite. Its great advantage over celluloid was that it could be moulded when hot into any shape, whereas celluloid had to be shaped by machines. In England, James Swinburne took out a patent for an identical substance, only to find Baekeland had beaten him by a day. Swinburne instead formed the Damard Lacquer Company to make paints; doubtless the name expressed his feelings. In America, bakelite was used to make junction boxes and distributor covers for cars, knobs and insulation in wirelesses, cylindrical phonograph records and countless other objects. British industry took no more interest in plastics than it had in synthetic dyes before 1914, and only wartime shortages taught both government and industry the importance of the new materials to replace the more traditional ones. American and German firms had a long lead in plastics production. Swinburne began to produce objects after the war and a number of other firms also began, often with government encouragement. Car manufacturers were good customers, and wooden electrical plugs and sockets were replaced by bakelite fittings. Even so, the industry grew slowly until 1932. Few types of plastic were known and even those had limited uses. Total world production was estimated to be no more than 80,000 tons in 1930.

Rapid expansion came soon afterwards. The synthetic rubber referred to already was in use for tyres and petrol hoses by 1934. The year before, polythene was invented by ICI scientists, though it was not until the war that a practical use was found for it in insulating radar cables. PVC, invented in Germany, was also used for insulation and for 'rubber' gloves, while the rigid kind was made into pipes. Another ICI invention, perspex, was used in aircraft during the war.

The sudden rush of new plastics necessitated different processing machines. Two main processes served for most products, extrusion and injection moulding. Italians had made spaghetti by extruding flour paste through a suitably shaped nozzle in 1800, and an American John Hyatt, had used a similar device in 1869 to produce celluloid rods, which then had to be machined to the right shape with saws and lathes. The extrusion of PVC pipes in the 1930s marked a new development, for the pipe was completely finished as it left the machine. A change of die (the 'nozzle') made a different shaped pipe, or a length of curtain rail. Injection moulding was more akin to metal casting, though much quicker as plastic hardens quickly. The molten plastic was forced into the closed mould, which opened almost immediately with the finished bucket or model aircraft kit. The raw materials also changed. In the nineteenth and early twentieth centuries plastics were derived from limestone, alcohol, cellulose and coal. Between the wars, coal became the main source, while America began to use crude oil in the late 1930s since that contained all the necessary chemicals. In Britain, Shell began to use oil to make polymers in 1942, and large plants were built after the war, such as those at Billingham and Wilton.

World production reached 400,000 tons in 1940. The industry then grew fast during the war to replace as many imported raw materials as possible. After the war, the various firms had the capacity to make large quantities of plastic goods and had to find outlets for them. Many things were made of plastic from 1945 to 1950 but too many of them were made from the wrong plastic, and did not stand up to use. The public were not prepared for plastics either and did not know their limitations—no one told them not to put plastic plates in the oven, for example. Plastics earned a bad name as a result, and 'plastic' meant 'cheap and nasty' to most people. Nylon stockings and toothbrushes, both popular and available by 1950, gradually persuaded the public that some plastics were better than the traditional products they replaced. Polythene buckets, bowls, dustpans and brushes were lighter and brighter than zinc and enamels, while polythene bags and bottles revolutionised packaging. Both public and industry came to accept plastics in the 1960s. Nylon gears were used where silent running and no oiling were needed; nylon rope and medical stitches were other uses. Polythene was made into drain-pipes, and the fashion industry's use of rayon, nylon and tery-lene has been noted above. Polyurethene improved varnishes, and polystyrene foam for cushions and insulation improved comfort. The search for new plastics continued, though not all could be developed because of the high costs involved. The transformation of everyday life brought about by the pheno-menal growth of the plastics industry cannot be underestimated.

17 Bricks, Books and Bottles

It is not possible in this book to relate the twists and turns of all industries, and pride of place has been given to the key industries in the country. The major industries were also the largest employers for most of the period treated in this section. There were, of course, many other industries. The growth of the population and of overseas markets allowed a much wider range of goods to be made, and these goods were made from components drawn from many industries. Contrast the nineteenth-century locomotive builders who constructed the whole locomotive from sheets and bars of metal with the twentieth-century factories where cars are assembled from components supplied by the electrical, engineering, rubber, plastics, glass and other industries. Some of the smaller industries are very small in terms of the numbers employed but their products are a necessary part of daily life.

The Victorians staged the Great Exhibition in 1851 to show to Britain and the world the quality and variety of goods made in British factories. The exhibition was partly a shop window and partly an attempt to boost morale after a very difficult fifty years. The long wars against France that ended in 1815 had been followed by many violent changes. There had been serious unemployment which persisted into the 1840s and many families had been forced to move into the industrial towns, where housing was both bad and expensive to rent, in search of work. Traditional work, such as the handloom weaving of cotton and worsted cloth, had been replaced by power looms in the mills, which needed fewer people to work them. Food prices were high because many harvests had failed; in particular, the continued

L

failure of the potato crop in Ireland (where potatoes were a staple food) caused a famine in Ireland—the decade is still remembered as 'the Hungry Forties'—which forced many people to emigrate to America, and hardship and a serious political crisis in England. Politically, the result was the repeal of the Corn Laws in 1846. Throughout the twenties, thirties and forties there was a great deal of political unrest, with riots and demonstrations (the most organised being those of the Chartists) which only died down with the economic improvements of the late forties and fifties.

Better times seemed to start with the railway building boom of the 1840s. Many men now had permanent work, either on the railways, in the factories making equipment or the construction firms. The cheaper and more dependable transport was an immediate encouragement to firms in other industries—coal could now be moved cheaply over long distances, for example, making possible the use of steam power on a larger scale than before.

The Society of Arts, presided over by Prince Albert, put forward the idea of an exhibition that would bring together the best from all round the world, the emphasis being on manufactured goods. The committee responsible for arranging it considered many designs for an exhibition building, and even tried to design one themselves, before settling for what must have seemed a futuristic idea. Designed by Joseph Paxton, the building was a vast greenhouse of iron, wood and glass, covering nineteen acres and allowing mature trees to be left inside when it was built in London's Hyde Park. Despite its size, the whole building was erected in less than four months. The amount of glass used soon earned it the name 'Crystal Palace'; contemporary critics were amazed at its size:

> Never in any other age or country, was such a sight presented as that at two o'clock on Thursday, October 7th, when 93,000 person were estimated to be under one roof at one time; and that not an open area, like a Roman ampitheatre, but in a windowed, and floored, and roofed building.

The building of houses, workshops and canals required large quantities of other building materials. These were mostly obtained by quarrying in the eighteenth century, and the lack of transport meant that most building was done with the local stone if it was at all suitable. This had the side effect of allowing buildings to blend with the landscape rather than clash with it. Many quarries were small and were cut into the hillside wherever a good outcrop of stone occurred. Great physical strength was needed to use the sledge and scabbling hammers, while gunpowder was used to bring down quantities of stone. There were also some areas where particular stone was quarried. Granite was popular in London for imposing buildings and bridges, and was taken by ship from quarries on Dartmoor, in the Lake District and around Aberdeen. A side industry in the latter region was the making of setts and kerb stones for London and other towns. Portland and Bath stone were also in great demand in many towns. Ralph Allen opened a quarry near Bath in 1727, and constructed a tramway to take stone to the boats using the river Avon which had been made navigable to Bath by the construction of locks. The railways delivered stone to all parts of the country in the nineteenth century, and Bath stone mines were started in the 1850s to keep pace with the demand. (Coal cutting machinery was adopted in one mine in 1945.) Roofing slates were also obtained from the immediate area wherever possible. Limestone could be split into heavy slates which needed substantial roof timbers, and such slates were used in the Cotswolds, and also Yorkshire and other areas. The thinner blue slates were quarried in Cornwall, North and South Wales, the Lake District and around Argyll and Perth. The Cornish quarry at Delabole had been started in Elizabethan times, and slates were taken by pack animal to fill boats beached at Port Gaverne. The widespread use of slates in the Midlands and London came after 1820, when the Welsh quarries were linked with the canal system.

Lack of transport prevented some areas from obtaining these materials and alternatives had been found. East Anglia had no useful building stone but its clays could be made into bricks and tiles. These were all sizes and many colours in the eighteenth century, for the makers were never quite sure how each batch would turn out after firing. Taxation at the end of the century led to standard sizes but discouraged the use of bricks. Those who had to use them, such as canal and railway companies, found them very expensive until the taxes were abandoned in 1850. Small brick yards opened wherever suitable clay could be found to meet the demand. Many used the traditional methods of making the bricks by hand but an extrusion press was brought into use at a Bridgwater yard and speeded up the process. Firing was expensive, for each batch involved heating the kiln from cold and maintaining the heat for some days, which consumed a ton of good coal per thousand bricks. Continuous kilns, built as a circle or square, came into use in the 1860s. The waste heat from one kiln was used to warm the next prior to firing; five hundred-weight of slack was sufficient per thousand bricks. The Oxford clay around Peterborough, which began to be used in the 1890s, and coincided with the start of large-scale cement production, contained some fuel in itself and reduced firing costs by a further third. This was enough to offset the costs of transporting bricks to all parts of Britain, and the rise of brick firms in that area was matched by the closure of yards elsewhere, especially in the 1920s–30s and 1950s. Three large firms were formed in the Oxford clay belt as a result of mergers which made half the bricks used in Britain; of these three the London Brick Company was the largest in the world. These companies reached their peak in 1965. The costs of transport and bricklaying and the availability of cheap alternatives led to a slow decline after that, and the local yards again found their more distinctive products in demand.

Timber for building was quite another problem and one which could only be solved by importing more and more. Attempts were made to economise as much as possible. Plywood came into use in the 1840s but could not be used outdoors because the glue made from boiled bones was easily soluble. Waterproof glues were developed for aircraft construction in World War I, and were steadily improved by the plastics industry. Plasterboard, chipboard and hardboard were other ways in which waste wood was utilised for building, and laminated beams were more economical than solid wood.

Greater quantities of glass were called for to keep pace with the house-building boom. Crown glass was the only kind of window glass available in 1750. The discs could be spun from forty to sixty inches across but could only make small panes and much was wasted. The French method of casting sheet glass on to a copper or cast-iron bed was started at St Helens by the British Cast Plate Glass Company in 1773. A Boulton and Watt engine was bought in 1789 for polishing and grinding. Yet another way of making window glass had been used in France in the fourteenth century but only started in England in the 1830s. This was cylinder glass, where a sphere of plastic glass was swung to and fro to form a cylinder which was then slit and flattened in the annealing kiln. This glass, made in Newcastle, was reckoned to be inferior to the other kinds. The industry had no marked expansion at the time of the industrial revolution for it was penalised by heavy taxation. This ended in 1845 as part of free-trade policy, existing glass firms expanded and new ones were formed. The price of glass fell by three-quarters, in 1844–9, and the repeal of the window tax in 1851 encouraged production still further. The Crystal Palace had a million square feet of glass on an iron frame.

The glass industry was one of the first customers for soda made by the Solvay process, using it in the 1870s. It also adapted reverberatory gas furnaces from the steel industry at that time. The production of wired glass in 1898 marked the start of making specialised goods. It was followed by glass bricks in 1900, toughened glass in 1928 and glass fibre for heat insulation in the 1930s. Plate glass continued as the main product, and this was speeded up when the float glass process came into use in 1952, with continuous casting over a bath of molten tin.

Glass was also needed for table use and packaging. The cutting and engraving of glass for fruit bowls and wine glasses reached its peak in the period 1760–1840. Those who could afford it expected to have glass on the table in preference to porcelain, and cut glass was very popular abroad. The rise in popularity of porcelain encouraged the glass firms to diversify into laboratory equipment and other specialist products, and very many table goods were made which were not decorated. At the same time, the need for bottles continued to grow. In the eighteenth century iron impurities made them black or dark green. Improvements were made to these low quality goods but they kept their green tinge throughout the nineteenth century. The popularity of waters from the mineral springs at such places as Cheltenham and Bath called for bottles, and the development of the mineral-water bottle with the marble stopper is a fascinating tale. Firms making ink, tomato sauce, smelling salts and a thousand other preparations all needed bottles, and the semi-automatic Ashley bottle making machine was in general use by 1900. This and similar machines used compressed air to blow the glass into shape within a mould, and the same idea was used to make inexpensive bowls and dishes. This side of the industry's output continued to grow but plastics replaced glass for many types of bottles in the 1960s.

Glass was something that only specialist firms could handle. Pottery, on the other hand, had always been a small-scale industry, developing wherever a usable clay could be found. Much domestic ware continued to be made by such potters well into the nineteenth century, and the use of salt glaze and slip as decoration became a distinct skill with many regional variations. The 150 potteries in the five towns that became Stoke-on-Trent were already larger than most in 1760, employing about forty people each. The local clay was adequate for everyday goods and the availability of coal was an asset. The great expansion of the Stoke potteries at the time of the industrial revolution was sparked off by Josiah Wedgwood, though many other eminent manufacturers came to be involved. Wedgwood was a characteristic example of the industrial revolution manufacturer. He opened the new Etruria Works in 1769 on the banks of the Grand Trunk Canal, which was still being dug, to make full use of the modern form of transport and reduce the horrific bills for breakages. He also experimented with new machines, though his experiments with glazes and designs were more far-reaching. The famous jasper ware became very popular, as were the fine table services and artistic wares. Wedgwood was soon selling to all parts of Europe, to Russia and America, and his goods were still bought in France after Napoleon banned all trade with England. Wedgwood also adopted business methods such as the division of labour, to allow people to specialise in a particular process. In this way his goods became cheaper—he not only supplied the most costly of dinner services but also produced the willow-pattern sets which more and more townsmen could afford. In turning his attention to making drainpipes, he was also anticipating the development of the sanitary-ware makers of the nineteenth century. The many firms that followed his lead brought about a complete change in habits for rich and poor alike, as silver, pewter, salt glaze and treen (wooden tableware) steadily disappeared from tables to be replaced by porcelain and mass-produced china, a process almost complete by 1939.

Mass production of paper had come rather earlier but was not part of the industrial revolution. Paper was still hand made in the eighteenth century; the ingredients were powdered cotton and linen, with some nettle stalks and similar plants. The pulping mills became larger as the need for paper grew, and were sited well up swift streams to have both power and clean water. Sorting the rags for paper was normally women's work and was very unsavoury. A seventy-two hour week in smelly, damp conditions brought in a wage of two or three shillings. Their work was gradually replaced by mechanical shredders and beaters. The Fourdrinier machine was developed at the beginning of the nineteenth century, and improved by Brian Donkin in 1803 and John Dickinson in 1809. The pulp was poured in at one end, drained and dried, and the paper reeled off at the other. Such machines needed both steam power and steam heating; large paper mills were set up near coal supplies, and many of the hand makers went out of business. The need for paper expanded rapidly in the nineteenth century, especially as a result of the penny post started in 1840, and the repeal of the newspaper tax (1855) and excise duty on paper (1861). The problem then became the shortage of raw materials—rags, waste from cotton mills and the like could not keep pace. Esparto grass began to be imported in 1857 but the real breakthrough was chemical wood-pulp. Pulp had been tried many times but the high cellulose content made it valueless. Boiling the pulp in soda removed the cellulose and the treated pulp came into use in 1873. The growth of the paper and board industries has been based on wood-pulp since then, though much board was made from salvaged waste paper after 1940 when the country temporarily realised it could not afford to throw everything away.

Hand-made paper was expensive, which discouraged any developments in printing technique in the eighteenth century. Printing workers were opposed to any greater use of machinery than already existed. Caxton would not have been bewildered had he entered a printing shop in 1750. Many changes came in the nineteenth century, however, as paper became cheaper and more people could read. The slowest process in printing was type founding. Even a skilled founder could do no more than six letters a minute, which meant ten minutes for a line. A type-casting machine was invented in America in 1838 and shown at the Great Exhibition. This was quickly adopted by the news-papers who had no time to sort type for re-use. Thirty years later type for *The Times* was made at 60,000 letters an hour. Setting the type was also slow, for the compositor had to select a letter at a time from a case containing ninety-eight characters and spaces. Henry Bessemer invented a Pianotype machine in 1842 which allowed two women to set 6,000 letters an hour but it was un-popular because of prejudice against women taking men's work. The Linotype machine, casting a whole line of type in one piece, was used by the major newspaper companies in 1900, and the Monotype machine, casting single letters, was adopted more slowly for setting books.

The presses used had not changed much in appearance since Caxton's day, though many improvements had been made. The Albion press that was in common use in the 1820s had a cast-iron frame and bed, and a single lever in place of the screw thread to press the paper to the type. It was still hand operated, and 500 copies an hour was hard work. A rotary press was invented by Richard Hoe in 1846, needing steam power. The newspaper companies adapted this to use a continuous roll of paper in 1865, which led to ever faster printing. Though constantly improved, rotary presses remained the backbone of the printing industry to 1970, and the volume of books and magazines printed continued to increase. The industry is an appropriate example of the im-portance of the smaller industries, for the influence of the printed word is considerable.

The manufacture of plate glass is displayed in the Pilkington Glass Museum, St Helens, and domestic glass is shown in Castleford Public Library and Museum, Brierley Hill Glass Museum, Dudley, and the Cecil Higgins Art Gallery, Bedford. English porcelain is also on show at the latter, and in the Wedgwood Museum, Stoke-on-Trent. The crushing of flints for glazes is shown in the Cheddleton Flint Mill, Leek, Staffordshire. Chair manufacturing is covered by the High Wycombe Art Gallery and Museum, Buckinghamshire, and a variety of crafts are displayed in the City Museum, St Albans.

18 Transport for Industry

The ability to move goods as well as people had always been important and industrial expansion made it essential. The growth of international trade required the fast and inexpensive movement of materials between factories and ports, and the use of components to manufacture complex products required similar facilities between firms within an industry. While road and water transport were improved at the time of the industrial revolution, these proved inadequate when industries expanded in the nineteenth century. Improved technology provided the answer in steam engines, which served all the needs of the basic industries. As these declined in the twentieth century a more flexible transport system was required, again using the roads.

About 400 turnpike trusts were in action by 1750, and were making an impact on the stretches of road in their care. The trustees were simply concerned to repair the roads they took over and make them passable for the normal traffic of the district. Some trusts were better than others but few attempted any drastic alterations to the roads. The number of trusts created accelerated after 1750, and existing trusts applied for new powers. This was in some cases to ensure a profit from the tolls but it also marked a second wave of activity by the trusts, broadly falling in the years 1760–90. The volume of traffic was increasing, especially iron, cotton and food, and there was a need for more wheeled vehicles rather than pack animals. The trusts therefore tried to ease gradients and to replace fords with bridges. Greater attention was paid to road surfaces, and engineers emerged who specialised in road construction. John Metcalf was responsible for several roads over the Pennines, while Thomas Telford surpassed all others by the number of trusts he and his assistants advised. Telford insisted that roads should have deep foundations, with stones decreasing in size towards the surface, where there was a covering of loose gravel. This made a good surface for a few months, but passing vehicles soon threw the gravel to the edges, and the bumpy foundations had to be re-covered. John Macadam devised a cheaper way of mending roads, using stones of an even size as fairly shallow foundations. The iron tyres of passing vehicles ground off chips which wedged between the stones and bound the road surface together. Macadamed roads were cheaper to lay and required less maintenance, and the idea was copied by the many trusts which Macadam advised. Not all trusts could afford the advice of eminent engineers, and some of those that could were loth to spend the money. Such trusts earned the strongly worded scorn of Arthur Young, a man who expected perfection, such as this in 1770:

From Newport Pagnel I took the road to Bedford, if I may venture to call such a cursed string of hills and holes by the name of road; a causeway is here and there thrown up, but so high and at the same time so very narrow, that it was at the peril of our necks we passed a wagon with a civil and careful driver. This is a pernicious and vile practice; it might be expected if thrown up at the expence of the farmers alone [i.e. a parish road]; but when found in turnpikes, deserves every unworthy epithet which frightened women or dislocated bones can possibly give rise to. [Arthur Young; *A tour through the North of England*, 1770.]

The volume of goods continued to rise and more people were on the move, leading to the final phase of turnpike development, 1790–1830. This period saw such major schemes as the Shrewsbury–Holyhead road which crossed the Menai Straits, and many trusts carried out reconstruction to allow wagons to travel faster. Better surfaces allowed coach builders to design lighter vehicles with better springing, which brought the speed of mail coaches to a time-tabled twelve mph, including stops for fresh horses. Only riding on horseback was faster.

However, turnpikes were only a small proportion (about 20 per cent) of the total mileage of roads even at their greatest extent. All others were the responsibility of the parishes, as laid down by the Elizabethan law. These continued to be maintained by statute labour until it was abolished in 1835 and replaced with a highway rate. Some parishes grouped themselves together, and were able to afford the advice of an engineer. The great majority did nothing of the kind and roads were as bad as ever. Wagons on such roads were the victims of endless delays, and firms sought other forms of transport.

This meant using the rivers and sea wherever possible. Parts of the Midlands and East Wales used the Severn, the rivers Mersey, Trent, Humber and Thames covered much of England, and the Clyde and Forth were heavily used in Scotland. Shorter rivers were also important—many industries were dependent on the Tamar, for example—and the navigation of quite insignificant rivers was improved by flash locks or similar schemes. Wherever possible, factories were sited within easy reach of these rivers, like the Darby works at Coalbrookdale on the Severn. Wagonways were built to bring heavy goods down to the river, especially to the Tyne coal staithes. Traffic using these rivers had also to go by sea from one river to the next, and the importance of this coastal trade was shown by the number of creeks that became harbours for the movement of such goods as the Cornish slates referred to earlier.

Rivers could not go everywhere, however, and hilly areas were obviously badly served. Yet it was in such areas that the new coalfields were opened up, attracting other industries in search of steam power. The need for transport in these areas became acute and the solution stemmed from a coal mine. The Duke of Bridgewater mined coal at Worsley, which was taken by pack animal to be sold in Manchester. Each animal carried two hundredweight, which meant that much time was spent filling the small pannier baskets. The duke knew he could sell more if it was cheaper, and engaged James Brindley to build a canal from the coal face for seven miles into Manchester. The aqueduct forty feet above the river Irwell was impressive enough but the fact that coal prices fell by half was not overlooked either. This was in 1761; Bridgewater had access to markets anywhere when he extended the canal to the river Mersey in 1767, and had to enlarge his mines as a result. The movement of bulky goods was much easier by canal as well as quicker, and these made it cheaper.

The idea was quickly taken up, and companies were formed to link the main rivers. The Grand Trunk Canal was opened in 1777 and provided a route from west to east by linking the Mersey and Trent. The Thames and Severn Canal was finished in 1789, and the Coventry and Oxford canals linked the Thames with the Trent. These canals made it possible to extend the range of boats normally using the rivers, and locks were made large enough to take ordinary river boats. In addition to these trunk canals, some far-sighted landowners realised what a boost being joined to the existing river transport system would be to industry on their lands. An example of this was Sir John Ramsden, who completed a canal in 1780 from the river Calder to his manorial corn and fulling mill in Huddersfield. Near the mill was some waste land where he developed an inland docks; this was a great stimulus to the woollen, chemical, brass and iron works already established in the town.

These early canals were all links with rivers. The success of the steam engine and consequent demand for coal began to make itself felt in the 1780s, and pointed the need for canals in areas far away from navigable rivers. Many companies were formed, particularly in 1792–4, to build canals linking the new industrial towns and mining areas. These were not intended for river boats but to be self-contained inland waterways. Most of them were constructed to take the seventy foot narrow boats, though some had local sizes of craft. Loaded boats could average two mph on these canals (smaller fly-boats managed $3\frac{1}{2}$mph) which was much faster and with a larger load than any wagon could manage on the road. Narrow canals in the Midlands and parts of the North of England were kept very busy with the needs of industry, though others in southern England could find little traffic. Canals were less effective than they might have been because of the difference between the two main groups of canals. A river boat was too wide to enter a narrow lock, a narrow boat too long to fit in a broad canal lock. Wherever canals of the two kinds met, as at Huddersfield or Stourbridge, goods had to be transhipped from one boat to another to continue their journey. This expensive waste of time was one of the factors that brought ruin to the canals.

Another was the steam engine. Many more wagonways were built in the period 1775–1825 than at any other time, to handle the extra goods. The canal companies built some to bring traffic on to their canal, and also to link canals through hilly areas. Other tramways were used to carry slate down the Welsh mountains, iron down the valleys and coal everywhere. The lines seldom linked with each other as they were built to take goods to the nearest water transport. The gauges used made linking even less likely, with anything between 4 and 5ft common in the North of England, 2ft in Wales and between 3ft 6in and 4ft 2in elsewhere. Availability of cheaper iron led at first to iron plates spiked on top of the wooden rails, and later to a great variety of cast-iron rails. Gravity was still the favourite form of motion but cable haulage up inclines was used, worked by water and then steam power. It was only a matter of time before the experiments of Trevithick, Blenkinsop, Hedley and Stephenson culminated in the use of locomotives as the only acceptable kind of power on the Liverpool and Manchester Railway in 1830.

The success of this railway far exceeded all expectations. Travel on it was more comfortable, faster and cheaper, and the stage-coach companieswere forced out of business in a year.The new use for railways, linking towns direct instead of in partnership with other forms of transport, was quickly copied. Dozens of companies obtained Acts of Parliament in the 1830s–40s, allowing them to sell shares and buy land, and the bulk of the railway network was completed by 1850. The frantic speed at which the railways were built was staggering, and all the more so in that this was the first form of transport to go faster than horses. The links between industrial areas accelerated the development of industry, and lines to the sea gave opportunities for day excursions. People, long accustomed to living their whole lives in one village, now began to move about, and in the towns they had fresh food brought in from the country.

The railway age lasted into the 1920s. Faster and more comfortable trains were developed, and signalling systems and the electric telegraph made travel safer. Few market towns were without a railway, and every village on a line had its station. The main traffic on the railways, however, was goods, and when these fell away in the depression years, the railway companies were in difficulties. The railways had been built when coal, cotton and iron dominated the industrial scene. As these declined and the newer industries grew up in other areas, the railways were left with a wasteful, inflexible system. Economies were tried in the face of competition from road vehicles. In 1923, 123 railway companies were amalgamated into four, and uneconomic branch lines were closed. Faster trains, special cheap fares and other attempts to boost receipts did not succeed in restoring to the railways their status as the only real form of transport. The railways were nationalised in 1947, and several attempts were made to make them profitable. The most drastic was the wholesale closing of unprofitable lines started by Dr Beeching in the 1950s, and the concentration on faster inter-city passenger services. Millions of pounds were spent on electrification and also on research into faster locomotives. Nothing seemed to tempt more goods traffic back from the roads, leaving the railways running at much less than full efficiency.

While steam revolutionised land transport in a space of twenty years, it took longer to adapt it to ships. Some steam ships were in regular coastal service by 1816, and on the Dover–Calais crossing in 1818. There were not many of them because the engines were expensive to buy and run. Engine builders began to make marine engines to new designs in the 1820s, and boilers capable of higher steam pressures economised on coal. Isambard Brunel took several long strides in ship design with the *Great Western* (1837) and *Great Britain* (1843). The latter was an iron ship, and better able to withstand the vibrations and weight of a steam engine. It was also driven by a screw propeller instead of the customary paddle wheels.

These ships only repaid the high building costs if they were used to carry passengers or mail. Wooden sailing ships were used for everything else, and ketches, brigantines, schooners and many others carried the growing volume of goods. The disaster rate was appalling, very few boats surviving to be broken up. Shipwreck was caused by all the dangers inherent in a ship driven by the wind. More sinister was the deliberate overloading of old and unseaworthy boats for which heavy insurance had been taken out, so that it did not matter to the owners whether they arrived or sank. These were called coffin ships and there were many of them until Samuel Plimsoll forced parliament to accept the Plimsoll line on all ships. This was a line painted on the side of each ship, which indicated the lowest the vessel could be allowed to float in the water; the compulsory adoption of the line made coffin ships impossible. Sailing ships carried the bulk of overseas trade, and also served the many coastal communities, collecting the products of the region and delivering goods and food from outside. This coastal and river trade was the life-line of many communities, for railways did not go everywhere. The ultimate in sailing ship performance was reached by the tea and wool clippers. These were of composite construction, an iron frame clad in wood and sheathed in copper. The largest could carry 2,000 tons and travel 400 sea miles a day in all weathers.

Iron cargo ships began to be built in the 1860s, when the compound engine had been developed which almost halved fuel consumption. Steel began to replace iron twenty years later. Its greater strength saved 20 per cent in thickness, which made ships faster and more economical. Steel girders meant that fewer supports were needed and large holds could be designed. This led to specialised oil tankers and grain ships, which no longer needed the goods to be packed in barrels or sacks. The size and range of such ships continued to grow, though compound engines gave way to steam turbines and oil engines. The coastal sailing ship and river barge continued to be important until the 1920s, by which time the coastal villages were being served by road transport.

This had been the undoing of the railways also. Large numbers of petrol-engined trucks were sold off as army surplus after 1918, and many haulage firms were started. There were also the steam wagons, which were more powerful and caused less pollution. These were built by Albion, Leyland, Sentinel and several other firms, and were widely used until the late 1930s. They were capable of faster speeds and heavier loads than were petrol lorries at that time, and could well have much to offer in the future.

Wagons and vans could provide a door-to-door service which the railways could not, and were quicker because they were more flexible. Road haulage took over most of the short distance traffic and bit into the rest, especially for the new industries setting up in areas remote from railway stations. Factories were built along the Great West Road out of London when it was constructed in the 1930s to take advantage of road transport. That road was the longest of the handful of new roads built before 1950.

The railway age of the nineteenth century diverted attention from the roads, which, outside towns, remained the responsibility of the parishes until 1888. Little was done by national or local government, despite the collection of motor taxes for the road fund, and the growing numbers of cars, vans, buses and lorries ran on dusty macadam roads. Roads had not been seriously designed or maintained since Telford's time, and it was probably beyond the resources of the country to bring them up to a standard suitable for motor vehicles within a few years. As a result, improvements like tarmac, road signs and white lines came long after they were needed. There was no national planning, nor was it ever decided how the conflicting needs of through traffic and local residents could be reconciled. After 1950, major road improvement schemes were started by many county councils, and the motorways separated some long distance traffic from the rest of the community. The first motorway, the M1, opened in 1959. The continuing rise in the numbers and weight of vehicles on the road caused the wholesale reconstruction of many towns, as well as pollution and damage to property. There was no national plan embracing all forms of transport, and consequently resources were not used to the full.

The efficient movement of messages has always been important to industry, for such purposes as the exchange of information about new products, and for the sending and filling of orders. The penny post came into use in 1840, and the Post Office took advantage of the railways to replace the mail coaches. The telegraph had been patented in 1837 but only became useful to industry when telegraph companies opened offices in the 1850s. These were taken over by the Post Office in 1868, by which time there was a cable to America as well as to all the

European capitals. Private companies and town councils began telephone services in the 1880s, which, except for Hull, came under the control of the Post Office in 1912. Later to be supplemented with telex, these provided a speedy way of obtaining components or spare parts for machines which made it possible for the complex inter-dependence of twentieth-century firms to work.

PLACES TO VISIT

There are more remains of transport than anything else and the following suggestions barely scratch the surface. Canal history is dealt with at the British Waterways Museum at Stoke Bruerne, Northants. Shipwrights' tools can be seen at Bideford Museum, Devon, and different kinds of boats at the Maritime Museum, Exeter, and the RNLI Museum, Eastbourne, Sussex. An interesting industrial harbour is in process of being put on show at Morwellham Quay, Devon, and visitors can go on the *Cutty Sark* in London and the *Great Britain* in Bristol. The Nautical Museum in Castletown, Isle of Man, is also of great interest.

Industrial railways are shown at Penrhyn Castle, Bangor, Caernarvonshire, and standard-gauge railways at Swindon and, from 1975, York. Many town trams can be seen and ridden on at Crich, Derbyshire. All kinds of horse-drawn road vehicles can be seen at the Aysgarth Falls Museum, Yorkshire, and motor vehicles at the National Motor Museum, Beaulieu, Hampshire.

A number of museums are concerned with several kinds of transport, such as the Transport Museums in Belfast and Hull, the Museum of Transport in Glasgow and the East Anglian Museum, Lowestoft, Sussex. See also those listed at the end of the book.

Conclusion

The physical remains of industrialisation are all around us. This is particularly true of Victorian and later activity but there is also a wealth of much older remains. The reader is recommended to seek out and explore such remains, for this will add a new and vital dimension to his understanding of industrial history. After reading so far in this book, no one should expect to have to travel to the Midlands or North of England as the only sources of industrial monuments. The agricultural regions that now seem remote from industry have seen thriving businesses come and go, which have left their mark. The 'places to visit' have been chosen to indicate how widespread these remains are.

Some monuments are exceptional, such as the bridge at Ironbridge or the *Great Britain* in Bristol. These stand out as major strides in technology and, for that reason, are not typical of ordinary industrial development. Examples of the ordinary must be sought in the local area, and there are few regions that cannot provide a good choice of illustrative structures. Smaller objects have been taken into museums, and are increasingly being used to display local industrial activity. Many of the industrial museums founded in recent years demonstrate processes. The sight of machines in action will give a clearer idea of how they work, and also how the workers had to work, than static exhibits can hope to do.

The history of industrial activity in Britain is very long. Some industries have had a continuous development, others have entirely disappeared, others again are recent additions. It is not always the oldest industries that are the best documented. Some firms have been thorough in the preservation of records, and a few have written their official histories. Others have few papers left, whether because of accident, wartime paper salvage or a lack of appreciation that a knowledge of past events can be both interesting and valuable. It is important that those who hold records either preserve them or invite the local museum to do it for them. This applies not only to written papers but to photographs, training and advertising films, catalogues, travellers' samples and so forth. It is impossible and pointless to keep everything but important that the valuable items should not be thrown away because of the storage problems created by a large volume of unsorted material.

The same argument applies to buildings and other sites. Some can be kept and found new uses, while others can make interesting features in otherwise featureless suburbs. Many must be demolished. The work of the industrial archaeologist is to survey and record such buildings, so that full details are available for future research. Many details of processes can only be explained by reference to the site or machine concerned and, where these cannot be kept, full records are vital. Details of local excavations and industrial archaeological societies can usually be found at the local museum, and are included in *Industrial Archaeology*.

Preserved machines, detailed records and visible remains are only the physical side of industrial history. The development of industry in Britain over the past 2,000 years is essentially a human story. It reflects man's need (and sometimes greed) for materials, for a living, for a way of protecting himself from the adversities of life and improving his comfort. I hope you will look at existing reminders of past industrial activity, and will think about the physical effort expended in creating them. Each generation builds on the work of others; its own performance, both good and bad, becomes the foundation of the future.

Museums

There are over 900 museums in Britain and nearly all of them have some exhibits to do with industry. The places to visit after each chapter should therefore be regarded simply as suggestions of the kind of place to explore. The absence of a museum from those lists should not be taken to mean that it is not worth a visit. The fullest information about the main items of interest in a museum is contained in the guide *Museums and Galleries*, published each July. Even this does not list all museums, so perhaps the best advice is to go and see for yourself.

Some museums contain much of interest about many industries, chief of which are the following:

Ulster Museum, Belfast
Ulster Folk Museum, Belfast
Birmingham Museum of Science and Industry
National Museum of Wales, Cardiff
Royal Scottish Museum, Edinburgh
Science Museum, London
Museum of Science and Engineering, Newcastle upon Tyne
Bridewell Museum, Norwich
Welsh Folk Museum, St Fagan's

Further Reading

The number of books available on various aspects of industrial history is very great. This list contains some of the more readily available.

General

Bodey, H. A. *Discovering Industrial History and Archaeology* (Aylesbury 1975)

Buchanan, R. A. *Industrial Archaeology in Britain* (Harmondsworth 1972), paperback

Chaloner, W. H. and Musson, A. E. *Industry and Technology* (1963), well illustrated

Derry, T. K. and Williams, T. I. *A Short History of Technology* (Oxford 1960)

Flinn, M. W. *Origins of the Industrial Revolution* (1966)

Hodges, H. *Technology in the Ancient World* (Harmondsworth 1970), paperback

Hudson, K. *Handbook for Industrial Archaeologists* (1967)

Journal of Industrial Archaeology

Jones, G. P. and Pool, A. G. *A Hundred Years of Economic Development in Great Britain, 1840–1940* (1940)

Mantoux, P. *The Industrial Revolution in the Eighteenth Century* (1961)

Raistrick, A. *Industrial Archaeology—an Historical Survey* (1972), paperback

Singer, C. and others. *History of Technology* (Oxford 1954–8), 5 vols

Thompson, E. P. *The Making of the English Working Class* (Harmondsworth 1968), paperback

Regional
(all this section published at Newton Abbot)
Ashmore, O. *Industrial Archaeology of Lancashire*
Atkinson, F. *Industrial Archaeology of North-East England* (1974)
Bawden, T. A., Garrad, L. S., Qualtrough, J. K. and Scatchard, J. W. *Industrial Archaeology of the Isle of Man* (1972)
Booker, F. *Industrial Archaeology of the Tamar Valley* (1971)
Buchanan, A. and Cossons, N. *Industrial Archaeology of the Bristol Region* (1969)
Butt, J. *Industrial Archaeology of Scotland* (1967)
Donnachie, I. *Industrial Archaeology of Galloway* (1971)
Harris, H. *Industrial Archaeology of Dartmoor* (1968)
Harris, H. *Industrial Archaeology of the Peak District* (1971)
Hart, C. *The Industrial History of Dean* (1971)
Hudson, K. *Industrial Archaeology of Southern England* (1965)
Johnson, W. B. *Industrial Archaeology of Hertfordshire* (1970)
Marshall, J. D. and Davies-Shiel, M. *Industrial Archaeology of the Lake Counties* (1969)
Nixon, F. *Industrial Archaeology of Derbyshire* (1969)
Rees, D. *Industrial Archaeology of Wales* (1974)
Smith, D. M. *Industrial Archaeology of the East Midlands*
Todd, A. C. and Laws, P. *Industrial Archaeology of Cornwall* (1972)

Mining
Barton, D. B. *A History of Copper Mining in Cornwall and Devon* (Truro 1968)
Ford, T. D. and Rieuwerts, J. H. *Lead Mining in the Peak District* (Bakewell 1968)
Griffin, A. R. *Coalmining* (1971)
Hall, G. W. *Metal Mines of Southern Wales* (Westbury-on-Severn 1971)
Jenkin, A. K. Hamilton. *The Cornish Miner* (1927, Newton Abbot reprint 1972)

Iron, Steel and Engineering

Armytage, W. H. G. *A Social History of Engineering* (1961)

Dunsheath, P. *A History of Electrical Engineering*

Gale, W. K. V. *Iron and Steel* (1971)

Greaves, W. F. and Carpenter, J. H. *A Short History of Mechanical Engineering* (1969)

Pannell, J. P. M. *Illustrated History of Civil Engineering* (1964)

Raistrick, A. *Dynasty of Ironfounders, the Darbys of Coalbrookdale* (Newton Abbot 1970)

Rolt, L. T. C. *Isambard Kingdom Brunel*, paperback

Rolt, L. T. C. *James Watt*

Rolt, L. T. C. *Tools for the Job* (1965)

Textiles

Bodey, H. A. *Textiles* (1975)

English, W. *The Textile Industry* (1971)

Heaton, H. *Yorkshire Woollen and Worsted Industries* (Oxford 1965)

Jenkins, J. G. *The Welsh Woollen Industry* (Cardiff 1969)

Jenkins, J. G. ed. *The Wool Textile Industry in Great Britain* (1972)

Lipson, E. *A Short History of Wool and its Manufacture* (1953)

Mann, J. de L. *The Cloth Industry in the West of England 1640–1880* (Oxford 1971)

Textile History (annual journal). Westbury, Wilts

Chemicals and Others

Anon. *Landmarks of the Plastics Industry* (1962)

Campbell, W. A. *The Chemical Industry* (1971)

Hudson, K. *Building Materials* (1972)

Jenkins, G. *The Craft Industries* (1972)

Kaufman, M. *The First Century of Plastics, Celluloid and its Sequel* (1963)

Shorter, A. H. *Paper Making in the British Isles* (Newton Abbot 1971)

Twyman, M. *Printing 1770–1970* (1970)

Power
Reynolds, J. *Windmills and Watermills* (1970)
Storer, J. D. *A Simple History of the Steam Engine* (1969)
Watkins, G. *The Stationary Steam Engine* (Newton Abbot)
Watkins, G. *The Textile Mill Engine* (Newton Abbot 1970)

Transport
Bird, A. *Roads and Vehicles* (1971)
Bodey, H. A. *Roads* (1971)
Coleman, T. *Railway Navvies* (1965), paperback
Cornwell, E. L. *Commercial Road Vehicles* (1960)
Larn, R. and Carter, C. *Cornish Shipwrecks* (Newton Abbot), 3
vols
Margary, I. D. *Roman Roads in Britain* (1967)
Maritime History (journal)
Morgan, B. *Civil Engineering—Railways* (1971)
Rolt, L. T. C. *George and Robert Stephenson*
Rolt, L. T. C. *Navigable Waterways* (1971)
Rolt, L. T. C. *The Cornish Giant* (Richard Trevithick)
Rolt, L. T. C. *Thomas Telford*
Simmons, J. *Transport* (1962), well illustrated
Snell, J. B. *Mechanical Engineering—Railways* (1971)
Transport History (journal)

INDEX

Index

Figures in italic refer to illustrations

207